"Only guard yourself and guard your soul carefully, lest you forget the things you saw, and lest these things depart your heart all the days of your life. And you shall make them known to your children, and to your children's children."

Deuteronomy 4:9

CHASED BY DEMONS: ©

How I Survived Hitler's Madness In My Native France

A MEMOIR

By

Jacqueline Grossman

Aventine Press

This memoir, **CHASED BY DEMONS**, is based on the author's recollection of events in her life prior to, during and following the Nazi occupation of France. It is supported in part by documentation from the National Archives in Washington D.C. among others.

ISBN:1-59330-599-0

Library of Congress Control Number: 2009931680
Library of Congress Cataloging-in-Publication Data

***

Designed by the author, the front cover of **CHASED BY DEMONS** features one of seven stone works that she sculpted in the 1980s titled, "Holocaust Echoes." The piece on the cover, "Furtively, We Three," symbolizes her flight from France in the dark of night, with her two sisters.

CHASED BY DEMONS:©
How I Survived Hitler's Madness In My Native France

IS DEDICATED

To Gary and Michelle and all the children,

Learn
Appreciate
Tolerate
Transcend

With Special Dedication To

My dear "little" sisters, for whom,

Out of the darkness of war that was your toddlerhood,
A time so filled with fear and bitter tears,
Memories could not flower as did in my childhood,
Warmed by suns of earlier blissful years.
Those living bouquets of cherished remembrances,
Still live in my heart, so sweet and so bright,
And fill my senses with exquisite heady fragrances.
Of lovely bygone days that do yet delight!
May the sunshine that nurtured my precious blossoms,
Brighten your days as you reach your lives' autumns.

Jacqueline Grossman

To My Reader

From My Heart To Yours

Ask: Can anyone who has not borne the terror and the agonies of war as a child ever understand how deep are the wounds, how gnawing and lasting the hurt, how haunting the memories?

This book reveals the life of the little French girl I was, during World War II. It is told through the eyes and heart of the child that still lives in me, but with the added perspective of the adult that those years made me become. It tells of the fears, the pain, the despair I experienced and of my search for ways to survive. It also tells of the loving family and the cherished childhood that were taken from me--and for which I still mourn.

It is also a personal memorial to those lost years, and to the stolen childhoods of all young innocents who survived, as I did, an insane period of history. I hope a better understanding can be gained of the transformations that occur in all children who grow up from times of war.

In my case, by virtue of the randomness of birth to parents who happened to be Jews, I became a guiltless, unwitting player during the world war of Hitler's Nazi era. Though I was spared the atrocities committed by Nazis against other Jewish victims (many of them members of my own family), in labor or extermination camps--I was nevertheless a Nazi victim. As such, besides profane humiliation, terror and hunger, my personal experiences were of wrenching separations and life-defining heartbreaks that have shaped what and who I have become.

When this traumatic period of my life was finally over, I tried to put it all behind me. In my teens, I never spoke of it. I felt I had no one I could trust with my grief and, most importantly, with my identity: a despised Jew. I was fearful of the consequences of such exposure--even in America. So, I rarely discussed my childhood--or my ethnicity.

As time passed, I could no longer bring myself to speak of those years. When I tried to respond to my own children's occasional queries, words would not come. Speech was inadequate for the shades of poignancy on the one hand and fury on the other that have ebbed and flowed deep within my heart over the years. I suppressed my story in the belief those years were behind me forever. But, "forever" was not to be.

In the closing decades of the twentieth century, I had come to be the only remaining member of my immediate family with first-hand knowledge of our story. Those who had been most closely associated with it were no longer alive. This gnawed at me. My children and my sisters' children had a right to know their background; I felt I owed it to them and to society to record that history. But how could I? I still felt vulnerable; I could not utter the words. My compulsion to hide was still too strong. For a long time, I battled these conflicting feelings.

But, need eventually overcame resistance. So I set about preparing myself for the daunting task of confronting my demons. Grief counselors might understand why, more than forty years after the war, it was through my rediscovered [1] artwork that the long suppressed emotional cleansing began. And the floodgates opened wide.

For the sculptor I had become, stone was an ideal medium. I worked alone, venting my feelings and reliving my pain. Through my hands, each strike of the hammer expressed my soul's hidden story. Rage was first to surface; its intensity took me by surprise. Deep sorrow soon followed and sobs echoed in the privacy of my studio while tears flowed unchecked as I retraced my defining years.

---

1 As a child, I had dreamed of becoming an artist but after leaving France, I was unable to explore my God-given talents until this period in my life.

Spontaneously and irrationally communicated through hammer and chisel, seven stone pieces emerged. Each gave shape to a different element of my wartime history. [2]

And I began to give chase to my demons. But, though the wrenching process had started, my voice could not yet release the words. So I turned to writing instead.

I was blessed with an exceptionally vivid memory of my childhood--days long gone but never forgotten. I was committed to recounting those memories as factually as I could and I wanted them seen in the context of the world events that shaped my life.

Much took place of which, as a child, I could not have been aware at the time. So, where practical, I researched events or revisited people and places, to verify or confirm. I scoured the works of historians--in English and in French--in order to place world events accurately in the chronology of my personal history.

The painstaking reconstruction of that history was an emotional maelstrom for me. But it was a storm I desperately needed to weather so that the crippling putrefaction of long-suppressed grief could be washed away.

This book is offered in evidence for the public record, in challenge to what some claim never happened. Here is one more piece of testimony of the black side of human nature that gave license to those years of darkness. Warring behavior must be shunned, the price is simply too great. What was lost in that war is tragically obvious. I believe its implications for the survival of mankind are not yet fully appreciated and must be earnestly examined and discussed.

I fervently hope this small work may contribute to such dialogue.

Jacqueline Grossman, 2009

---

2 One of those seven pieces is featured on the cover of this book. Entitled, "Furtively, We Three," it represents three faceless little girls, escaping the Nazi scourge into the night.

Ask: How will other young souls be transformed, whose childhoods continue to be sacrificed in unconscionable ways to man's brutality and insatiable lust for wealth and power? What price may we all pay when those children come of age?

Acknowledgements

This story could never have been written without the support, patience and empathetic ear of my loving husband, my soul mate of over fifty years. To him I owe more than words could ever say!

Encouragement came from many and diverse quarters. You know who you are. Thank you all from the bottom of my heart. During the final phase of the numerous edits and rewrites, a few individuals stand out above the rest however. I give special thanks to Bea and Nina. But, Jerry, Ruthe, Marilyn, Barbara and Jean shed light where it was most needed. Your knowledge of writing taught me much about giving chase to those demons. I love you all.

CONTENTS

Dedication   v
To My Reader: From My Heart To Yours   vii
Acknowledgments   xi
MAP-Occupied France, 1940-1944   xiv

PART ONE: CROSSROADS
    Chapter   I   1943 - The Oath   3

PART TWO: WHAT WAS LOST
    Chapter   II   The Beautiful 1930s   11
    Chapter   III Homes and a Stork   17
    Chapter   IV   Family Secrets   31

PART THREE: TRANSITION
    Chapter   V   The Nightmare Begins   41
    Chapter   VI   Adieu, Paris   57
    Chapter   VII Heading South, At Last!   73
    Chapter   VIII Luchon   89

PART FOUR: DESPERATION
    Chapter   IX   Dread and Pretense   101
    Chapter   X   Furtively, Three on a Farm   113
    Chapter   XI   The Dark Journey Begins   125
    Chapter   XII Darkest of Nights   133
    Chapter   XIII ¡Olé! ¡España!   143
    Chapter   XIV Adieu, Mes Amours   149

PART FIVE: WHAT WAS FOUND
    Chapter   XV   Mainsail West   161
    Chapter   XVI The New World   173
    Chapter XVII   The Legacy   191

Sources and References   203

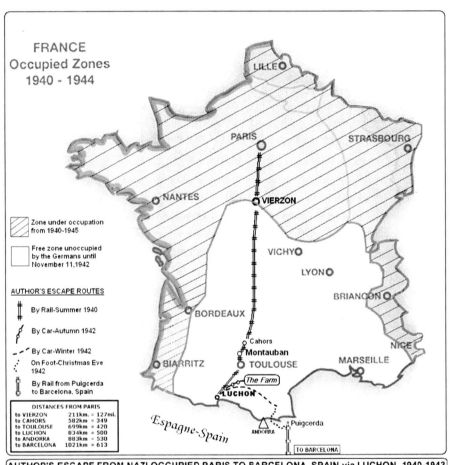

**FRANCE
Occupied Zones
1940 - 1944**

LILLE⊙

PARIS   STRASBOURG⊙

⊙NANTES   ⊙VIERZON

VICHY⊙

LYON⊙

BRIANÇON⊙

⊙BORDEAUX

Cahors
Montauban
⊙BIARRITZ   TOULOUSE   MARSEILLE   NICE
The Farm
⊙LUCHON

Espagne-Spain

ANDORRA   ⊙Puigcerda

TO BARCELONA

Zone under occupation
from 1940-1945

Free zone unoccupied
by the Germans until
November 11,1942

AUTHOR'S ESCAPE ROUTES

By Rail-Summer 1940

By Car-Autumn 1942

By Car-Winter 1942

On Foot-Christmas Eve
1942

By Rail from Puigcerda
to Barcelona, Spain

DISTANCES FROM PARIS	
to VIERZON	211km. = 127mi.
to CAHORS	582km = 349
to TOULOUSE	699km = 420
to LUCHON	834km = 500
to ANDORRA	883km = 530
to BARCELONA	1021km = 613

AUTHOR'S ESCAPE FROM NAZI-OCCUPIED PARIS TO BARCELONA, SPAIN via LUCHON, 1940-1943

CHASED BY DEMONS

PART I

CROSSROADS

CHAPTER I

1943 - The Oath

"Swear." Her face ashen, Maman struggled to maintain self-control. But I could hear it; the strain in her voice betrayed her agony.

With patience and love, she had told me that fate sometimes gives us no choice and forces us to make great sacrifices. That was how she had explained the latest turning point in our lives that now put me in this unbearable position.

"Swear." She asked again.

I could not respond.

"Please give me your word, Darling." Maman implored.

Silence.

"Jure, Chérie." "Swear, Darling."

"Jure sur ta tête …," she repeated, despair now rising in her voice.

I looked up at Maman. Her beautiful round face, framed by mid-length wavy black hair held back over each ear with a small tortoise comb, was pale and distorted with grief. Her usually smiling brown eyes now reflected anguish.

"Swear on your head, that God may strike you dead if …" She grasped my shoulders and warned gravely, "… if you let anything happen to your little sisters."

Icy fear gripped my heart when I heard those words and I began to tremble. I knew that God was all-powerful. Maman had told me so many times, that it was a bad thing to make Him angry. I could not speak.

Her breath caught. Waiting for my reply, she choked back a sob.

All the while she probed my terror-filled eyes with her own beseeching ones, and waited for a hoped-for reassuring response.

When still none came, she raised her voice, "Swear!"
More silence.

She tightened her grasp on my shoulders, her fingers digging into my flesh, and shook me violently. Her voice shrill, she now commanded,

"SWEAR!"

But I stood frozen. I was terrified. No sound could come from my throat for I believed with every fiber of my being that a positive response to my distraught mother would most assuredly bring God's unimaginable wrath down on me. I felt incapable of carrying out Maman's demands. So how could I take this oath?

Maman's resolve suddenly shattered. No longer able to maintain any semblance of self-control, the flood of tears she had barely kept in check now overcame her. I watched horrified as she fell to her knees, racked by sobs.

"Jure, Ché-r-i-i-e-e ... Je t'en suppl-i-i-i-e-e ..." "I beg you," she wailed as she wrapped herself around my waist and buried her head against my chest.

For what seemed an eternity and while her sobs echoed in my heart, I fought back my own tears and the terror that held me in its grip. In reality, that terror lasted merely a moment. But it was a moment frozen in time, a moment that has haunted me ever since.

I felt helpless, trapped ... and so overwhelmed. How could I, an eleven-year-old, be a maman? *Je ne veux pas... Je ne veux pas... I do not... I do NOT want to do this*, my soul screamed.

I must have gone into a mild state of shock. Small rivulets of sweat began to run down the sides of my face and down my spine; yet, I shivered. Each time I opened my mouth to speak, my throat constricted and no words would form.

My eyes reached out to my mother, imploring, *Non, Maman. Please don't make me swear. I can't do it. I'm too little. I'm frightened.*

All at once my head began to spin. I felt queasy. And where did that loud drum come from? Then in a moment of clarity I realized it must be my own heartbeat thumping in my ears.

Stop that! I scolded myself silently.

Suddenly, I experienced an odd feeling, a sense of time standing still or of things moving in slow motion around me. A little voice was making itself heard in my head over the din of my heart; it counseled reasonably from the deepest recesses of my mind. *Sois brave. Be brave.* It said. *You are the oldest; you can and you must set the proper example for your little sisters. Hasn't Papa always told you how strong and smart you are? You should be able to do this.*

Despite this admittedly compelling logic, I was not convinced. My thoughts raced through the ghastly possibilities that lay ahead if I took the oath my mother demanded of me. *What if ... Oh, horrors! What if I failed?*

I had visions of my little sisters lying dead somewhere because I, and I alone, had failed them. I could see an avenging Jewish God, angry and disappointed with me, cast the ultimate penalty: a gigantic thunderbolt that would snuff me off the face of the earth in a flash. I could see myself an outcast in some forever after Jewish purgatory, banished from everything I knew and loved, while this bereaved and broken woman, my mother, pointed an accusing finger at me for all eternity.

For what did, indeed, feel like an eternity, I stood transfixed staring down at my sobbing mother begging me to take this crushing oath. I watched as she cried out in grief and despair to what she called a merciless God who was forcing her to send her children far away from her. Why, she asked, did God put her in the untenable and soul-searing position of choosing between their possible capture by a demon of an enemy, or, sending them away from her to live in a foreign land on another continent without knowing when, or if, she might ever see her children again … in order that they might escape the Nazis, in order that they might live?

Her words and the memory of that horrible day still haunt me.

Despite my initial resistance, this terrifying oath was finally wrested from me. *"Oui, Maman. Je te le jure."* I, at last, quietly and gravely swore.

I understood. There had been no choice given me by my mother or by circumstance.

That day, by putting the lives and well being of her three children in my hands, Maman made me her eleven-year-old surrogate. This daunting mission was now forever etched in my soul. But, having given my word, I was determined to succeed. I remembered what Papa always said about promises being sacred. So, I felt compelled to do my utmost to honor the oath I had taken. The lives of my two sisters depended on it, as did my own. Had I not sworn on my life? Would God not strike me dead if I did not keep my oath to Him and to my distraught mother? So, in the span of a few wrenching moments, the precious little that remained of a once bright, exhilarating childhood slipped away forever.

I quickly learned to rely on the finely honed survival instincts I had developed since the invasion of France, nearly three years earlier. Somehow in the trying years that lay ahead, I found the strength, the maturity, and the wisdom I needed to carry out my "mission."

In the process, though, I lost a great deal that is precious and natural to children: laughter, lightheartedness, and the ability to trust the world. Overnight, I became a sober, intense, and watchful child with a compulsion to hide her ethnicity, a child who could never again savor the carefree innocence or joys of untarnished childhood.

As young as I was, I understood full well that Hitler was responsible for our shattered lives, and I felt outrage at being chased away from my home by this demoniacal Nazi leader. I also knew that my parents were powerless to stop him. But the outrage I had felt against this madman since our escape from Paris three years before, now metamorphosed into a more complex mix of emotions.

When I first learned that, for our safety, my sisters and I were to be sent overseas, I tried to dissuade my parents from sending us away. I presented what I thought were compelling arguments. Like a grownup, I argued that children should be with their parents. But, they--especially Papa--would not reconsider.

Within my soul, a new gnawing sense of loss took root--so deep that for a long time it eluded definition. The anger I had felt for many months now mingled with an overwhelming sense of powerlessness, grief, and yearning for what was rightly mine. I had lost my home, my friends, my childhood and the country I loved. And now I was losing my parents. These losses became too much to bear.

My lifelong grieving had begun. But added to this were new seeds of resentment. Now, along with my rage at what I believed was an unjust Jew-hating world, resentment also began to grow against my parents.

"You must be the mother now!" Oh, how that phrase kept me awake nights for a long time to come. After all these years, and long after her death, my mother's words still echo in my mind, "You must be strong … you must be..."

I wanted so much to run away from that responsibility. How I longed to hear her say that she had not meant what she had asked of me, that it was all a horrible nightmare from which I would soon awake. My heart yearned to be back in those safe wonderful days of my childhood, to be back in Paris before the War, before the bombs, before "Dirty Jew" echoed in my homeland.

Before Hitler!

CHASED BY DEMONS

PART TWO

WHAT WAS LOST

CHAPTER II

The Beautiful 1930s

Paris! That magnificent city of light, of love, of beauty and of excitement was my birthplace. And, for the first nine years of my life, it was also my home.

I loved everything about it. I delighted in the busy noisy *marchés* where Maman bought our meat, fish, and vegetables fresh from the farm or from the sea for the day's meals. I adored the *boulangeries* with their warm, crusty fresh bread and tempting pastries. Our local *boulangerie* was where Maman had me take her roasts, neatly tied, spiked with fresh garlic, buttered and seasoned to perfection, to be baked in its big ovens for a few *sous* (we had no refrigerator or oven in those days).

Then there were the *charcuteries*. From their windows, roasted pigs' heads smiled, inviting us to enter. Inside these cool shops--with their clean white marble counters and tiled floors--mysterious mouth-watering smells announced to all that fresh ham, *pâtés,* and a myriad of other delicatessen treats were sold there.

The sounds of Paris enchanted me! I loved the clippety-clop of horses' hooves on the cobblestones of narrow side streets, and the unmistakable 'nei-ei-ei-gh … pffp-pleunfff' of an upstart horse asserting itself. Such sounds always announced the arrival of vendors, hawking wares and services. These street merchants made regular rounds on horse-drawn wagons well into the 1930s.

There was the *chiffonier* selling and buying rags, "*Chiffons, Mesdames. Chiffons."* He yodeled up toward the many windows of our apartment building.

And there was the unforgettable *marchand de glace* garbed in white. A burlap bag, folded with one corner cleverly tucked into the other to create a hood, was draped over his head, shoulders and back. Always bent on timely deliveries and a short workday, he greeted his chatty customer with, *"Attention Madame. Laissez-moi passer, j' vous en prie."* (Let me pass, please.) A large pick firmly gripped in hand, he harpooned an enormous block of ice out of the rear of his white wagon, heaved it onto his burlap-draped shoulders, and quickly carried it dripping into Madame's waiting icebox on his weekly customer route.

Also part of the steady stream of vendors was the soot-covered *charbonnier* who delivered our anthracite *charbon*. Cellar coal bins had to be filled regularly for the pot-bellied stoves in the many old, stove-heated apartment buildings above, where central heating was too costly an improvement to make.

Occasionally, troupes of colorful gypsies came from nowhere in brightly decorated carts and show-wagons drawn by bejeweled, plumed horses. The jingle and jangle of their bangles, beads, and bells mingled harmoniously with the brilliance of hand cymbals and clacking *castagnettes* held in graceful hands. Dancers twirled and swirled dizzyingly to the sound of lusty guitars and the passionate *vivace* of gypsy violins.

A steady creaking sound routinely announced the large wooden wagons that came daily to collect the fresh manure left behind by all the great hoofed beasts that regularly roamed our city streets. The characteristic aroma that lingered was a silent reminder of this unsolicited but highly prized commodity sought by French farmers who always preferred nature's way.

There also the rolling crunch of the *rémouleur*'s knife-sharpening cart pushed along residential side streets; its owner lustily calling, *"Razoirs, couteaux, ciseaux,"* (Razors, knives, scissors) up to housewives who, with equal vigor and consummate skill, negotiated the best deal from their upper story apartment windows. Soon, the metallic whirr of the grinding wheel, responding to the thumpety-thump of the foot pedal driving it, signaled that a deal had been struck.

I was occasionally lucky enough to be down in our courtyard--at a prudent distance--when the sharpening of a large utility or carving knife began. Showers of gold, blue, and white sparks shot forth to both thrill and intimidate me. When this fireworks show was over, I would approach the cart to take a whiff of heated metal that mingled with the tanning smell of the full-body leather apron worn by the sharpener, before its owner pushed his crunching cart on to the next courtyard.

There were other sounds too. The shrill whistle of the *gendarme* was repeatedly heard on busy streets because it somehow never quite captured the attention of its intended audience. Its owner, blowing on the shiny little mouthpiece gripped between his teeth, conducted traffic with balletic abandon. Occasionally he stopped, *"Alors, vous êtes sourd?"* "So, are you deaf?" he shouted to a heedless driver. In the thirties, the upstart automobile was already taking over Paris. The loud throb of its engines and brazen "oohgah-oohgah" of its bell-shaped horns blended with the impertinent "drrring-ring-ring" of the Parisian's beloved bicycle. All of this was punctuated by the shouted insults of automobile drivers who, even then, ignored traffic rules and settled differences their own way.

I also loved the music--from the accordions and violins in *cafés*--music that seemed to float through the air on Sunday afternoons while we strolled, Papa, Maman and I, on *les grands boulevards*. These walks were Sunday rituals. I would ride on my Papa's shoulders when I was a toddler, and, when I was a bit older, I walked between Papa and Maman while I hung on to their hands, at times swinging off the ground, pretending I could fly. I remember looking up at these two "giants" who pulled me along, begging to be allowed to ride on my *papa's* shoulders again and again so I could see my city and all its happy people enjoying as I did, the sights, the sounds, and the ambience that were so uniquely … Paris!

Around four o'clock in the afternoon I was given a crusty *tartine au beurre* (a piece of baguette spread with sweet butter), or a fresh, flaky, just-out-of-the-oven *petit pain au chocolat* from one of the pastry shops on the boulevards. On other occasions, it might be a hot *cornet de frites*, the inimitable french-fried potatoes that were prepared and sold on major street corners all over Paris and handed to us in a paper cone fashioned out of yesterday's newspaper. How I adored *les frites,* crisp and crunchy on the outside and buttery soft on the inside. Yum! They were never in the paper *cornet* long enough for the fat, still sizzling on the sides of these delectable little golden sticks, to generate more than a few interesting oily patterns on the outside layer of paper that absorbed it.

Also cherished in my memory is the newspaper stand on every street corner where dozens of papers for every conceivable ideological and political point of view were displayed. These were the lifeblood of Parisians who, while they drank their morning *café-au-lait* or afternoon *apéritif* at the corner *bistro,* were continually engaged in heated discussions over local and world events.

In the autumn and winter, the trees that lined the boulevards stood majestically barren in silent promise of robust green glories to come. The days turned cold and crisp and the skies were often gray.   At such times, the wonderfully comforting aroma of roasting chestnuts filled the air.

I was mesmerized by the sight of these brown treats roasting over hot coals in big soot-covered metal drums. I stared at the red and blue flames that could be seen dancing through vent holes in the drums' sides. Bundled up and hooded against wind and cold in several thick layers of clothing, red-nosed vendors tended them carefully. I watched as they deftly slit each chestnut with a small knife, and gasped when their nimble fingers--nearly touching the hot pan above the burning coals--danced lightly over the nearly done ones to turn them.

My mother often treated me to these *marrons chauds.* Holding them in a *cornet*--the same kind of paper horn used for *les frites*--they warmed my cold hands while I trudged happily beside my *maman*. They were oh so tasty. Nothing, not even the heavily laden skies of a cold Parisian winter day--or the newsboy hawking his papers who might occasionally be heard calling out something about a young Fascist German leader named Hitler--could dampen my spirits.

On a more mundane level, something else stands out vividly in my mind, the metal *pissoir*. I noticed this smelly convenience at an early age. Found at strategic locations along the boulevards, this in-and-out precursor of today's public pay-toilet was provided free--for the needs of men only! As a little girl, my analytical and critical thinking skills were often at their peak during moments of urgent personal need. At such times, I wondered if those who were powerful enough to create such practical solutions as the *pissoirs de Paris*, were under the impression that little girls and their mamans never needed to go *"pipi."* But I don't recall ever getting an answer to this most pressing of questions. When my needs peaked and my abused bladder insisted, I just had to settle for the usual, *"Maman, j'ai envie."* (Maman, I need to go!) Whereupon we'd walk to the nearest café to buy a *limonade,* thereby earning the right to use the establishment's *W-C* (double-V C, water closet toilet).

And this, too, became the stuff--and smells--of cherished memories.

Others come to mind: *Le Petit Guignol* puppet shows in the park. And the organ grinder's little monkey dressed in his cute red bellhop uniform with matching cap, striking the brass cymbals clutched in tiny fingers with eyes darting nervously between his master and his audience.

We also made occasional trips to the circus to admire all of its wonders: trapeze artists, clowns, magicians, colorful costumes, and animals the likes of which I had never seen before. I remember, too, the magical cotton candy that went from pink fluff to sticky stuff in one lick. This wet red sugar always ended up decorating my outfits and the bench I stood or sat on before I could finish it.

Sometimes we strolled along the *quai de la Seine* to look at all the vendors' stalls, the artists at work, the lovers wrapped in each other's arms, and the boats that drifted lazily down the river. It felt so grownup when we stopped to check the poster-covered *kiosques* (kiosk) to see what new *spectacle* or performance might be of interest. How could passersby know that I, at age four, was merely pretending I could read the fine print, just like Papa and Maman?

We often stopped at a *café* on the left bank in the late afternoon. I'd sit on a chair dunking my flaky butter croissant in a cup of hot milk, or sipping cocoa from a spoon with my dribbling chin barely clearing the table, where a small brown puddle would inevitably collect. There was always an instrumentalist performing in the *café*--an accordionist or a violinist; sometimes there was a singer too. Maman loved this music. She often hummed or whistled along; she trilled and whistled so well. Everyone who heard her said that she sounded just like a bird. She and Papa smiled a lot and spoke almost cooingly to each other in those happy days.

Oh, how I loved my city, … my home!

CHAPTER III

Homes and a Stork

The first home I remember was a small, somewhat dark, second floor, two-room walk-up apartment on the *rue de l'Entrepôt*. I was only a toddler but I recall how proud I felt to be able to climb the narrow circular staircase to our floor. Maman held my left hand firmly, and I steadied myself against the dingy beige wall on my right while I triumphantly lifted one leg at a time above waist-level to clear each step. Of course, Maman did help a little.

When I was three or four, we moved to the condominium apartment that became our "permanent" home--until the Nazi occupation. To me, this apartment was a "palace." Its seven rooms were spacious, with lots of little places in which I could play and hide. It was on the fourth floor of a sandstone block building that must have been perhaps two-hundred-years-old. As there was no elevator, furniture and equipment were pulleyed up outside from the courtyard below and eased in through the tall French-door style windows of the condominium apartment. The building had been upgraded where practical with electrical conduits as well as plumbing and sewer pipes that were attached to exterior walls. Its age notwithstanding, it was in great condition. I loved the views. From the living room, I could look out onto the large cobbled courtyard below, and from the rear, intriguing rooftops spread out as far as my eyes could see. I could not have been happier there.

The heavy iron *porte cochère* that gave motor-car or horse-drawn wagon access to and from the street below was closed and locked every night at ten o'clock by the concierge. But built within one of the nail-studded garage-size portals was a small pedestrian door for use when the larger double carriage doors were closed. On the interior side of the *porte cochère* was a broad, covered passageway. The large cobblestone courtyard then opened up beyond to reveal a few garages against high sandstone walls that delineated the properties on either side of the courtyard. I imagined our iron portal had welcomed many fine horse-drawn carriages into this courtyard in earlier times. Our apartment building was at the quiet far end.

When we returned late in the evening from an outing with family and found the *porte cochère* locked, my father pressed a little white button next to the doorframe outside; after a few seconds, the small pedestrian door clicked open for us to step in. I was convinced it was magic. All Papa had to do to complete this mysterious ritual was identify himself to the concierge--a faceless woman who assumedly sat behind a darkened window taking note of who went in and out.

"Simon!" he called out his name as we walked through the portico and past her ground floor apartment window. Everyone knew Papa by his first name because it was also the name of his company, *Établissements Simon*. Each time I walked past that window, I wondered, with the many occupants who checked in late at night, if that poor concierge ever slept.

Having thus passed muster, we would walk quickly in silence (so as not to wake anyone sleeping) to our wing at the far end of the courtyard where, on moonlit nights, our shadows slunk along at our heels. I was convinced a bogeyman lurked in the dark, so I always made sure to be between my parents during these unnerving little walks.

By the time we reached the building entrance and the few sandstone steps that were worn down from centuries of use by countless feet, my fright was at its peak. A pitch-black stairwell awaited us. Three long flights had to be climbed in order to reach our home.

To light the way, an archaic but most frugal timed electrical system had been installed. I was given the task of pressing its timer button at the bottom of the stairs to activate it. However, the timing mechanism had been set very precisely for adult use. The lights always went off just before I reached the next landing. Unless Papa or Maman hurried ahead to press the next button, we were thrown into utter blackness. Chills ran up my spine while we felt our way along the wall to that all-important little button for the next set of lights.

Despite these turn-of-the-century shortcomings, I loved our condominium apartment. The high-ceilinged rooms were large and airy. Thanks to the very thick walls of our building, windows had recessed spaces that created an ideal place to hide behind curtains and play house or *Cache-cache* (hide 'n seek). As an added bonus, the sills were low enough for me to be able to see the large cobblestone courtyard below and the treed garden of the courtyard next door. Lovely ornate wrought-iron railings with wooden balustrades graced each window of our building. I loved to climb up onto the sill and lean far over the railing so that I could look straight down onto my courtyard. I still have a vivid, not very pleasant recollection of the whipping Papa gave me when I was not quite five for doing "such a dangerous thing." Why didn't he understand that I had everything under control?

Personal hygiene and laundry needs were addressed inelegantly but effectively. Plumbing consisted of cold running water in the kitchen, a "water-closet" toilet just off the foyer-- the kind with a ceiling tank and a pull-chain--but no bathtub or shower. These modern conveniences had not yet graced our building.

Like most other people who lived in Paris' numerous older buildings in the 1930s, we were quite adept at sponge bathing. Maman had an oval aluminum tub in the kitchen--used only for our personal daily washing--which we filled with hot water from a large kettle heated on one of the gas burners. For real bathing, we went to one of the numerous bathhouses in the neighborhood. The one we frequented also had steam rooms and a pool, and you could even get a massage if you had the means. The bathhouse was a weekly treat to which I looked forward with immense pleasure.

As for laundry, Maman did the light wash in the kitchen at home with the special tubs she kept for that purpose. First, she boiled the laundry in soapy water in a cast aluminum tub on the counter-top gas burner. After the soapy water had cooled, it was an easy matter to scrub off whatever dirt remained before she began the numerous rinses in cold water. Then, the clean laundry was hung outside the kitchen window on a pulley line to dry. Heavy-duty washes such as linens were taken to a commercial neighborhood laundry.

From the windows in the back rooms of our apartment, overlooking the rooftops of Paris, I saw my first Eiffel Tower *feu d'artifice* fireworks that commemorated *le jour de la Bastille* each year on July 14. What a beautiful and exciting spectacle it was. And we had a grand view of it.

However, my friend Henriette upstairs had an even better one. I was thrilled when I was invited there to play. It seemed as though we were on top of the world or airborne, so we often pretended to be aviatrixes or parachutists. Henriette was a little older than I, but we got along famously. She and I, with her little brother, played a lot together at our favorite game, *hôpital.* She would be the doctor who took my pulse, tapped on my chest and back, and gave the nurse (her brother) orders for the patient's care. Hmmm … I frequently wondered why did I always end up being the patient and never the doctor?

When Henriette came downstairs to my home, however, we played house. I had the perfect place for this game in the dining room under the sleek mahogany dining room table. We could sit comfortably on the thick Oriental rug that graced the hardwood floor. There, we made believe we were entertaining little friends with Maman's lovely Limoges porcelain dishes and silverware just as she often did with her own friends. But of course this real finery was off-limits to my destructive little fingers and was safely locked up in the china cabinet. At times of such games, I was naturally the all-important hostess and Henriette was merely the guest. After all, she was the visitor and didn't know her way around my imaginary dining room house. This room was a special playroom for me. Large and airy, I spent a lot of time there. An imposing fireplace occupied nearly half of one wall, while beautiful family portraits graced the other walls. Besides the elegant mahogany table and matching china buffet--with its beveled glass doors and mirrored back wall that reflected the crystal's thousand twinkling lights--there was a new upright piano. It flanked the tall French windows in one corner of the room, and a floor-model Victrola record player was in the other. A mysterious little ritual with the turning of a metal crank on its side was all this Victrola needed, and it played the sensuous, *"Le plus beau de tous les tangos du monde, c'est celui que j'ai dansé dans tes bras..."* ("The most beautiful of all the tangos in the world is the one I danced in your arms...") that Maman adored. She played it so well on the piano. Tangos were very popular in those days. When I was alone, I tried to play just like she did. The far-from-melodic sounds that resulted never prevented me from trying again and again. I simply pretended I was hearing beautiful music.

There were forbidden places I loved to explore in our big home. In the front room that served as office and reception room, Papa's enormous roll-top desk was an exploration paradise. I was certain its many little drawers and cubbyholes held forbidden treasures simply waiting to be discovered. Since, on Sunday mornings I was the first one up, these were perfect times for my secret before-breakfast treasure hunts.

Papa's mysterious workrooms, also off-limits, drew me like magnets and were too tempting for me to resist sneaking into when Papa and Maman were too busy to notice. When I could, I gingerly opened the sewing room door to gape in amazement at Papa's whirring power machines that seized unrecognizable pieces of fabric and spat them out in rapid-fire succession as perfect ready-to-wear garments. Another wondrous sight awaited my curious eyes in the cutting room. There, sounding like a hive of buzzing bees, the power-cutter hummed throatily while the technician guided it deftly along pattern lines, cutting through dozens of fabric layers stacked one upon another as easily as if they were a layered cake.

Ah, yes! What a marvelous exploration playtime paradise this home was. Whether make-believe or real, I always found lots of fun things to do there.

My friend Henriette's family was Catholic. At Christmas time, I was invited upstairs to participate in the family's festivities and gift giving. Their beautiful Christmas tree was decorated with dozens of real little candles that burned down to their tiny clip-on holders every night. I knew our family could not have a Christmas tree because we were Jewish and the Torah only knows of a burning bush. But I was allowed to believe in the *Père Noël* (Father Christmas) and to accept the gifts that he brought down our dining room chimney when I had been a good little girl. I even had my own *Père Noël papier maché* doll. This tall slender figure--the much healthier French version of Santa Claus--also had long flowing white hair and a white beard, but he was dressed in a floor-length trailing gray robe trimmed in what was meant to resemble ermine fur. He brought me a beautiful porcelain doll one year and my first tricycle another year. I couldn't wait to compare gifts with Henriette.

What an innocent, sweet, wonderful time it was.

Many other friends filled my early years. When the weather was nice, Maman took me to a small neighborhood park a few blocks away where many other children were brought to play as well. In the center was a large pond surrounded by a wide gravelly path. Nannies guided their leather perambulators on that path amid the laughing, squealing children who played there. Many of us had large wooden hoops that we pushed along rhythmically with a wooden *bâton* to keep them rolling as we ran alongside. All the while, mothers and nurses sat watching from green wrought iron benches strategically placed on the grassy area that ringed the path--some were knitting while others read or chatted with neighborhood friends. Occasionally, women's voices rang out cautionary warnings to their charges, *"Marcel, ne cours pas trop près de la rue."* Or, *"Fais attention à ton blouson Émil; tu es tout prêt de l'eau."*

Most days, many little wooden sailboats floated lazily on the pond, their colorful sails catching just enough breeze to push them along. Little boys, often dressed appropriately in sailor suits, waited impatiently at the edge of the pond for their boats to reach shore so they could push them "out to sea" once more.

I had no such beautiful sailboat. Little girls were not normally given boats with which to play. Their toys were of the more feminine sort such as dolls and miniature carriages. But, the adventure of the sailboat drifting off to visit faraway exotic places, or to fight battles against pirates, set my imagination on fire. So, it wasn't long at all before I made friends with the lucky owners of such boats.

"Si tu me prêtes ton bateau, j'te laisse jouer avec mon cerf-volant… (If you let me play with your boat, I'll let you play with my kite…), I bartered. Soon, I had a small fleet of sailboats at my disposal in exchange for the loan of my colorful *billes* (agate marbles) or for my wooden hoop or kite.

In time, I had a loyal following, mostly boys. We met to play, first in the park, later in the street outside my apartment building, and ultimately in my courtyard. My preference was for boys' games as far back as I remember. So, the majority of my outdoor chums were boys. But I still loved to play indoors with girls and with dolls if the circumstances and the weather made this a more appealing option.

I was always inquisitive and perhaps overly imaginative. Never at a loss for some exciting new play adventure, I soon became the undisputed leader of my little band of five-year-olds. I remember many thrilling adventures of jungle safaris in the park, and narrow but successful escapes from pirates on the pond. Most memorable was a pretend parachute jump with an umbrella from a garage rooftop in our courtyard--a would-be catastrophe nipped in the bud by my watchful father upstairs and for which I, as ringleader, was soundly spanked.

The autumn following this episode, I was enrolled in Kindergarten at *École Béranger,* the school just up the street from our home. Boys and girls were segregated in adjacent buildings, as was then the custom. And that was the end of my little band.

Some time during that year, I had my first major early childhood heartbreak: I was forced to confront the crushing truth about that benevolent seasonal personality, *le Père Noël.* A girl I knew in school, who seemed to delight in being the bearer of bad news, shared a grownup secret with me one day that left me devastated.

"There is really no *Père Noël!*" She declared with more than a tinge of malicious pleasure. I could almost see her smacking her lips, like a wicked witch.

"But how can that be?" I retorted. She must be wrong, I thought. Somebody, after all, had come down our chimney, I argued.

"I have proof; he left me presents!"

"But you never really saw him, did you?" She challenged with unmistakable scorn.

The logic and finality of her gleeful explanations, uncontested by my maman when I ran home crying, were inescapable. I was devastated and inconsolable. What a black day that was!

However, after that initial shocking loss, I kept my grief to myself and soon found something positive in this tragedy (my first lesson in turning a liability into an asset). I could now lobby directly for all the toys I wanted at *Noël*--I pressured Maman, herself. What newfound power! Nevertheless, from that point forward, I despised the little girl who had been the bearer of such painful news and I avoided further contact with her. She had, after all, torpedoed an important element in the magical world of my childhood. I wanted no more bad news!

So, I turned my attention to more important things. I became a serious student, earned high marks and received several school awards. Papa was very proud of me. He bragged to Maman that none of his friends' children was being recognized--he probably bragged a lot to those friends too.

#

Though I was otherwise a happy child with many friends, at some point, I decided that I needed a little brother or sister. Why? Well, sometimes--especially in winter when I couldn't go out to play, and Henriette was not available--I was lonely. Besides, I thought it would be fun to have someone to boss around a little. After all, what good is a leader without someone to lead?

But, how did one go about getting a little brother or little sister? I had no idea. Naturally, I decided to consult Maman on this matter. Being wise beyond words, she should certainly know how to go about such things. And, indeed, she knew exactly what to do.

"Il faut mettre un morceau de sucre ... You must put a lump of sugar out on the window sill *pour la cigogne."* She counseled. "And if the stork comes for the sugar, that means she will then bring you a brand new baby."

No, she did not know if it would be a boy or a girl. That was the stork's secret.

So, as I was advised to do, I carefully and dutifully placed my sugar lump on top of the *garde-manger* window box cooler that was mounted outside onto the kitchen window frame. This covered box served as our family's butter and cheese cooler.

Since its top was large enough to hold two big plates, I was convinced the stork would most certainly want to land there to rest. She would then not fail to see my sugar and would pick it up, I reasoned.

For several weeks, perhaps months, I checked the top of the window box faithfully every morning. Much to my chagrin, the sugar was still where I had placed it. I began to lose heart. Then, after a time, I stopped looking altogether and turned my attentions elsewhere.

But, one day, Maman said, *"Regarde, Jacqueline, Chérie.* Look! Your sugar is gone!"

She beckoned with a broad smile on her face. I scrambled up onto the chair to peer over the top of the window box. I held my breath; my heart was beating so… Yes! Yes! YES! The stork had come.

Finally, I was going to be someone's older sister. This business of being an only child had its merits, true, but let's face it; it gets pretty boring just talking to yourself when you play "let's pretend." Besides, everyone else I knew had siblings. Now, I too would finally have my own little fulltime friend to play with. I couldn't wait.

#

So, it came to pass on a cold drizzly evening in February 1937, that Maman took me shopping at the *Magasins Réunis* for my very own baby buggy. It was something for which I had longed ever since Christmas, two months earlier, when I'd received a new porcelain doll from my now-pretend *Père Noël*. I loved this beautiful doll whose heavily eye-lashed, demure blue eyes opened and closed so beguilingly. When I tipped her forward, she cried, "Ma-a-ma-a-a!" It stimulated my nurturing instincts to hear her cry, so I tipped her forward a great deal. Besides, then, I could tell her to be quiet!

I was so proud to be grown up enough to have a baby of my own; I took the responsibility very seriously. I combed her silky hair, bathed her, changed her panties when she soiled them, and scolded her for doing so. My new buggy was perfect for her; I took her for walks to the park (up and down our hallway), to the market (in our kitchen), and rocked her buggy in my bedroom to help her *faire dodo.* After all, I had to practice for the real baby soon to come into my life.

About a week or two following the purchase of my new baby buggy, Maman took me to my Aunt's home--with my doll and buggy of course--while she went to pick up my new baby sister from some mysterious place where storks deliver their bundles to waiting mothers. She said I could not remain at home while she was gone. I had planned on meeting the stork. I was vexed to be left out of this part of my deal with the elusive bird that had eaten my sugar without letting me know when or where we would get our new baby--or that I could be there when she dropped it off!

So, to soothe my ruffled feathers, Maman said I was to help name our new baby. Although I was still miffed at the stork, I accepted this task with the greatest pride. I promised Maman I'd give it my utmost attention.

She was more or less true to her word on this matter. "Eveline" was her choice for the baby's first name, whereas I had chosen, "Mireille." But, since she was the Maman, I grudgingly let my vote be the weaker of the two, and I settled for the middle name. Thus, Eveline Mireille was born on March 1, 1937.

Seventeen much-busier-than-I-expected months later, on August 14--to my great surprise and without any coaxing or sugar bribes from me--the stork delivered Paulette, my second sister. But, this time, I did not receive the news with boundless joy.

I was already sharing Maman with my first sister who, by the way, was not the kind of playmate buddy I had expected. She required tedious supervision from me when Maman was otherwise occupied. I felt betrayed by the stork for not giving

me a ready-to-go playmate and had decided I would not give it
any more sugar ever, ever again! So, why did it leave us another
baby? Could it be, I wondered, that another stork had felt left
out and had decided to get even with me for not giving it a treat
as well? If so, it was not only a surprise, it was a dirty trick on
the part of that vengeful stork. I did not relish the thought of
sharing Maman with any more needy sisters.

Yes, it was quite a surprise. But then, as I recall, when I
asked Maman if she or Papa had put out a lump of sugar, she
said no, they had not. So it must have been a surprise to Maman
and Papa as well.

That was how it came to pass that in the summer of 1938,
Eveline and I were sent to the country to stay with a *nourrice*
(wet nurse), a common practice in those days among the middle
class. This *nourrice* continued to nurse Eveline while Maman
gave birth to my new baby sister. It was a difficult birth and
Maman required surgery, so we remained in the country for the
rest of the summer and early fall.

This *nourrice* and her family had a small farm in *Montfermeil*,
a little town near Paris. We were allowed to go wherever we
pleased on that farm. As city children who spend so much time
indoors, this was quite a treat, for I loved to run and explore.

I have a vivid recollection of a wonderfully mysterious wine
cellar there. It smelled at once musty and fruity and was o-o-oh
so refreshingly cool during the hottest days of summer. Wooden
kegs, mounted on special stands, lined the walls. Their spigots
were perfectly placed for ease of use--by the two of us.

These tempting stopcocks reached Eveline at eye level and
intrigued her so. She was an inquisitive toddler by now. The
spigots turned so easily in her little hand. What fun toys! With
a simple twist of the hand, they magically released a tasty, cool
and refreshing, deep purple elixir.

Although I was already old enough to merit a glass of *"eau
de vin,"* (the mix of water and wine that I was now privileged to

have at mealtime), Eveline was still too young. However, she must have learned to like it when she was teething. At those times Maman had gently placed pieces of baguette drizzled with wine between her sore gums. The baby had always quieted down at such times. Eveline had apparently learned to like it a great deal.

Since she had already been introduced to wine, I saw no reason for us not to visit the *nourrice*'s small wine cellar during our play times away from the main house. I must admit, though, a few *soupçons* (hints) of doubt did creep into the deepest recesses of my mind that, if we had asked, Eveline might not have been given permission to turn so many spigots on and off--standing under them with mouth wide open as she went!

Ah, what a wonderfully fun place to explore--in between giggles. And explore it we did, at every opportunity!

However, during rare moments of sober reflection, I couldn't help but wonder what my strict Papa would have said had he known.

CHAPTER IV

Family Secrets

I owe so much of what I am today to my parents, who they were and the decisions they made during some of the darkest hours of my life, that I need to share what I know about them and how they came to marry in Paris, before I continue.

My father, Sender Grossmann, was born in Kamionka Strumilowa, Austria on November 10, 1898. This "*shtetl*" village was twenty-four miles northeast of Lemberg (Lwow) in the East European district of Galicia, a border province of the then Hapsburg Empire. At the time of his birth, and since 1772, this region was partitioned from Poland. Due to its strategic location, its borders have changed countless times and it has flown the flag of many nations. Though my father was officially born an Austrian, the language and culture of his district remained predominantly Polish and he considered himself a Pole.

Coming from a relatively poor family, he left school and his home at the age of thirteen, following his Bar Mitzvah (the Hebrew coming of age ceremony of thirteen-year-old Jewish boys), to seek his fortunes westward. His dream was to immigrate to the United States. Starting in Lemberg, he trekked across Europe for several years, working at various jobs to earn enough money so he could try to realize that dream. He remained in each country to work only long enough to save enough money to be able to leave it.

A resourceful young man, he had the courage of a lion and keen survival instincts. He was quick to take advantage of opportunities that came his way, or to manufacture a few if they didn't.

At the beginning of World War I, while in his mid-teens, Papa was at his most creative as a vendor of contraband goods to

German soldiers. One such illegal item was champagne, highly prized by officers who were willing to pay handsomely for it. Papa was young, hungry, and desperate. He had no suppliers for this expensive elixir; so, he "created" his own. He obtained empty champagne bottles from upscale restaurants where he occasionally washed dishes and, *voilà!* French Champagne for sale!

What the officers purchased from him was truly foul. Given his intense dislike of Germans, he had taken great pleasure in filling each bottle by pissing into it.

Unsurprisingly, this youthful enterprise resulted in his being sought by a number of extremely irate customers with murder in their hearts. However, by the time they had discovered the true nature of their purchase, he had accumulated enough cash to move on to a new region in search of unsuspecting new prospects. But, his notoriety quickly preceded him; his customer base totally vanished and now, many of the Kaiser's soldiers were in hot pursuit. Never mind new regions; it was time to move out of that country altogether, and he did so ... with haste.

Eventually, he made his way to the Netherlands. There, for a year or two, he worked near the docks. From the stories Papa told of himself, he was something of a rebel as a teenager, with a pugnacious penchant. Scrappy conflicts were not infrequent. On one such occasion, at eighteen while he was working in a meatpacking plant, he got into a fight with a meat-hook-carrying bully. It caused him the loss of an eye. [3]

Still intent on emigrating to the West, but unable to afford regular passage or obtain immigration documents, my father attempted to stow away several times aboard vessels bound for the United States. He first tried from the Netherlands, then from

---

3 It was only after his death in May 1962, that I learned from my mother of his prosthetic glass eye. A very proud man with a giant ego, he had sworn her to secrecy; she was to tell no one about it while he was alive. She, herself, only learned of it by accident early in their marriage when she came across a prescription for it in his coat pocket.

northern French seaports where he was twice discovered hiding under the canvas covers of lifeboats. Finally, his dubious luck forced him to rethink his strategy and select a new destination.

So, in 1922, he headed for Paris where, relatives like his Uncle Stein (who had immigrated several years earlier) could provide a helping hand. To fit into the mainstream business community, Uncle Stein advised him to change his given name from Sender to Simon--a familiar first or last name in France-- and to remove the last 'n' from his surname. He did as he was advised. Now, it was time for Simon Grossman to settle down.

Notwithstanding his questionably ethical beginnings as a teenage entrepreneur, Papa had a natural gift for business. He had a quick mind for figures, an analytical one for reducing complexity to relative simplicity, and he was a gifted negotiator. With a fierce determination to achieve, nearly boundless energy, and winning ways with customers, his success was assured. He took great pride in what he later accomplished as a mature and honorable French businessman.

Eventually, he built up what began as a small leather goods business into *Établissements Simon, Fabriquant de Vêtements de Cuir et Imperméables*, a successful rainwear and leather outerwear manufacturing company. But this did not come about until after he had found the right woman to be by his side.

#

It was in Paris that Papa met Chana Mindla Gielčmann. (The family's surname was later changed to Gelsman and she adopted the first name of Anna, an easier one for the French to pronounce). She was to become his wife and, later, my Maman.

The second youngest of five children, Maman was born in 1902 in the *shtetl* village of Konskie, Poland. Not long after the outbreak of World War I in 1914, the family moved to nearby Lodz. There, she showed early promise in school. Not only did she excel in standard subjects, she had an exceptional facility for languages and an outstanding memory. Later, she demonstrated a natural gift for music and art as well. Her high grades paved the way to high school admission--despite the State's minimal Jewish quota allowance. Few children were formally educated beyond the age of thirteen in those days; they went directly into vocational apprenticeships. So, admission to high school was more than a special achievement for her as she was the only child in her family to attend and graduate high school. This distinction also gave her access to a wealthy social class. Her numerous high school friends came from families of certain means and standing in the community. Through them, she acquired culture and sophisticated tastes.

She graduated with distinction. Her teachers strongly urged her to pursue a higher degree, something she also wished for herself. But, her family could not afford it, and Poland's state scholarships were rarely if ever awarded to Jews.

Besides, by this time, Poland's political and economic climates had deteriorated dramatically. Massacres of Jews were frequent and their lives became particularly difficult. Maman's parents decided to leave Poland. However, she stayed on with an older sister, working for lawyers in the town's courthouse. But, after a couple of years, she, too, left and followed her parents to Paris where they had settled. She was nineteen at the time.

Maman had still hoped to go to law school when she arrived in France, but her parents didn't have the means to send her to the University there either. Instead, she enrolled in business school and eventually became a certificated stenographer.

She immersed herself in the intricacies of shorthand and the stylistic flourishes of French business syntax. In a relatively short time, Maman's command of the French language nearly rivaled that of her native tongue.

That was how Maman, a promising young Polish girl, became, as she relished calling herself, *une française*. In that great capital of learning, culture, and fashion, it was an easy and most welcomed transition for this beautiful young woman with a thirst for knowledge, a flair for style, and the social skills to pave the way.

In Paris, her social needs were well met, especially in the popular *"dancings"* (ballrooms) of that city's flapper era. There, *la coquette* Anna who loved to dance and flirt, could show off her grace, her beauty, and her charms.

No wonder Papa took notice. He fell in love with her the first time they danced. He thought she was a prize for any young man and he wined, dined, and wooed her until she could no longer demur.

He and Maman were married on March 26, 1929.

#

Papa was good-looking himself as a young man, and he was a dapper dresser. It was always apparent to me that he, too, had a sense of style, expensive style at that.

I remember when we went out to visit relatives, or for a Sunday promenade, he looked so handsome. His expensive suits were made to measure in the latest fashion and fabric of the day, with matching spats. (The spats had dozens of tiny round black buttons that required a special hook for Maman or me to pull through equally tiny buttonholes.) To complete his outfit, he draped a silk scarf inside the neck of his perfectly fitted overcoat, and a Homburg hat was tilted ever so slightly to one side on his head. Fine leather gloves were held in one hand while on the little finger of the other was a diamond ring, his mark of success.

All this elegance was topped off with a touch of expensive men's *eau de toilette*. And, when he lit up his favorite *Gauloise* cigarette, that he had snugly fitted into a smart tortoise-shell cigarette holder, his hands with their freshly manicured nails were as perfectly groomed, as well matched, and as polished as the rest of his person.

#

I was born on August 21, 1931, the first female child of three consecutive disappointments for my father who desperately wanted a son. As a man who was raised in the most traditional of old-world Jewish cultures, he valued boys far more than girls. He frequently made that clear; even my nickname, *Jacquot*, his idea, was a boys' diminutive.

When I did something he thought clever or when I came home from school with an award, he would say to me, "*Ah, ma petite Jacquot, Chérie.* If only you were a boy, we could accomplish such great things together, you and I." I came to know this left-handed compliment by heart. I could even sense the statement coming before he uttered its first word. Although it was his way of saying he was proud of me, and in a strange way it flattered me, it nevertheless made me angry. To me, it really meant, "Since you're only a girl; you'll never be good enough." Each time he uttered those words, my resentment grew. It was a reminder that no matter what I did, I could never meet his standards.

These comments not only offended and hurt, they were frustrating. I was absolutely convinced I could be as good as a boy and could have made his chest swell with the same pride if only he would give me the opportunity to prove it.

"I can do the same things a boy can do. Let me try." I would plead. But he would not change his mind or give me the chance I asked for. I could not convince him to allow me, a mere girl, to be the offspring by his side. Although I felt a sense of personal power and self-confidence at an early age, my father was a man who could not accept such qualities as valuable ones in a mere daughter.

Nevertheless, he continued to take great pleasure in my childhood accomplishments. All the while, though, he continued to groan about the great things he could have achieved with me by his side if … "*Mein Gott, Jacquot. Si seulement* … if only you had been a boy!"

Yet, in his way, he truly did love his family of females. Notwithstanding that love, his mercurial, Napoleonic nature was rarely hidden for long. Maman's family, with some justification, considered him something of a tyrant. He ran his household with an iron fist. In his home, we were expected to do his bidding without challenge. He ruled; we obeyed. No questions asked. He also believed in corporal punishment, and he insisted that Maman apply it as well.

Until I was old enough, big enough, and strong enough to physically defend myself, he disciplined me only too frequently. Although I respected and loved him, it was a respect and love interlaced with fear.

I grew up resenting his ways and his unequivocal hold over my mother. Treatment by this highly control-driven man caused me to vow never to allow any man to exercise that kind of power over me when I grew up--including him. Nevertheless, I do realize that the independence and determination that prompted my secret vow were qualities I undoubtedly inherited from him. They were probably what helped me to become the survivor I became in the difficult times I would soon face.

CHASED BY DEMONS

PART THREE

TRANSITIONS

CHAPTER V

The Nightmare Begins

It is very cold. Yet, in a bizarre sense, it is warm. I am running, alone and frightened, lost in a maze of dark green shrubbery. There is no moon, but some mysterious source of light from above gives shape to my immediate surroundings. Melted snow glistens on the shrubs. I have never seen such shrubs before. What are they? The leaves are small, stiff to the touch, and shiny. And I sense unseen tiny red blossoms or berries without distinct shape here and there.

The maze seems endless. For a moment, I stop running. Which way should I go? My palms are clammy. I feel trapped.

There! I hear it again! A frightening snorting sound that sends chills down my spine. What is this terrible monster whose presence I feel but cannot see? Is it looking for me? Is that why it sounds so near despite my efforts to get away from it?

There it is again! I start to run once more. He's close; I can hear the thump-thump of many footsteps. Terror grips my heart. How many are there? I stop and listen hard. No, there's only one; but he has so many feet this monster. I hold my breath. He seems to be sniffing nearby. Now I'm sure he's hunting me. I press myself into as small a shape as I can and hunker down under the shrub.

I gasp! Oh no, he's there on the other side of my hiding place!

It is now or never. I inch forward in the shadows looking for a way out. Ah! I see one. But it's so far. I don't know... can I make it?

I wake up screaming, drenched in my own sweat. I am in my bed, safe in Paris.

It is summer 1939.

#

Little did I realize how much this terrifying nightmare I had as an eight year-old foreshadowed events of the following three plus years.[4] It may have also set the stage for what later became my near-compulsion to hide my ethnicity.

Every day, newspapers now carried headlines of trouble in one eastern European country or another. The Russian revolution, toward the end of World War I, had brought about major changes. It had given Communism a strong toehold in Eastern Europe and its influence was moving westward. Western leaders became more and more concerned as hungry people, dissatisfied with their economic fortunes, agitated for change.

Scapegoating against defenseless minorities became commonplace; blame had to be placed somewhere by central European politicians if they were to maintain political control of the masses. There were organized massacres of innocent people--especially Jews--in countries like Poland and Russia. These pogroms, as they were called, soon gained acceptance in Germany as well. Under the fanatic leadership of Adolf Hitler, a new doctrine, Fascism, surfaced. Now, in Germany, scapegoating against Jews reached new heights. By blaming Jews and claiming the Aryans a superior race--which appealed greatly to the German ego--Hitler was able to keep the restless working class under control.

The mass exodus of east European Jews to the west was a predictable outcome of their unchecked persecution following World War I. These early emigrants fairly quickly found niches for themselves in Western Europe where they were able to eke out modest livelihoods. But as the migration went on well into the 1930s, France began to watch all central European developments anxiously. French concern was increasing, not

---

4 Years later, I learned that other young, would-be victims also experienced never-forgotten vivid nightmares that foreshadowed events to come in their lives--as this one foreshadowed a critical Christmas night for me.

only over mounting pressures on the country's economy, but also over the growing possibility of another war.

#

One mid-autumn afternoon, Papa and I were on a bus returning home from visiting relatives. We were standing on the small, canopied boarding deck at the rear--my favorite place to ride the bus. From there, I loved to watch the blue-uniformed conductor pull his bell-chain to announce the stops en route.

While the bus made its way down the boulevard, I put my face over the railing defying the stinging chill of the autumn wind that whipped my face and blew my hair every which way. Although the trees had stopped exploding with seasonal reds and yellows, many colorful leaves still clung tenaciously to branches. I remember thinking how beautiful it all was. I felt so alive and happy.

In my hand, I held a new red satin ribbon that Papa's friend had given me that afternoon. *What a nice flag this would make. It could be flown over big important buildings,* I thought. Clutching one end of the ribbon tightly in my hand, I put it over the railing and watched it proudly wave in the wind.

"Regarde mon drapeau, Papa. What a glorious flag!"

Suddenly, almost brutally, Papa yanked my arm back. "Do you want people to think we're Communists?" and he swiftly pocketed my ribbon out of sight of glaring eyes.

"We'll get arrested," he hissed angrily

"Why? What did I do wrong?" I asked in a pitiful little voice, my chin beginning to quiver.

"It's not you, *Chérie."* His voice softening as he leaned over to whisper, "It's what Hitler and the Russians are doing. It has made French people nervous." And he explained that red was the communists' color. It was then I first sensed that something had changed, had gone terribly wrong in my world.

Things had indeed changed ... far beyond my ken.

It was now late Fall 1939.

#

The political turmoil in Eastern Europe had significant impact in France. It brought about the ban of the French Communist Party in September 1939 following the signing of the Nazi-Soviet non-aggression pact in late August. The French government was now also applying severe punitive measures where necessary in an effort to stem an advancing Red Tide on its own soil.

Also in September, honoring its pact of alliance with Poland and following the Germans' invasion of that country, France had declared war against Germany. Things were looking very bad indeed.

#

My father now often had a frown on his face. He listened to all the radio newscasts. He read dozens of newspapers every day. At the end of each workday, when he joined his friends at the corner *bistro* in the late afternoon for a round or two of *Belote (*one of his favorite card games), passionate discussions followed while they drank their usual *apéritif.*

During our traditional, French-style two-hour midday dinner, he reported the morning's news to Maman from the many papers he read daily. At supper, while the always-animated discussions he'd had at the corner *bistro* were still fresh in his mind, he reviewed the reactions of local Parisians to events in central Europe. My parents were seriously worried now.

At first, Papa conversed with Maman in French. When he realized I was hanging on to every word, he soon switched to Yiddish. But since I already had some grounding in that language, it didn't take long before I understood Papa's Yiddish reports as well. And I, too, became worried.

I asked a lot of questions about that monstrous man named Adolf Hitler who hated the Jews so much that he wanted to kill us. I was passionate about the subject and bombarded my father with questions.

"Why doesn't *Monsieur* Hitler like us? Why is he afraid of us? What have we done to him?"

One evening, after participating more than usual in the discussion, I had a sudden inspiration. I knew how to resolve the Jews' problems! I presented my idea to Papa.

"Put me on a train for Berlin, I will go by myself to negotiate with this wicked *Monsieur* Hitler on behalf of the Jews. I will say to him, 'I'm Jewish and you can see that I don't have horns.' I will smile sweetly at him and tell him, 'we're not monsters; we're actually very nice people who don't hurt anyone. There aren't even enough of us to make war or hurt anybody.'" With a sense of noble mission, I looked at my Papa squarely in the eye and declared, "That's what I will tell *Monsieur* Hitler."

I argued my case forcefully to my parents. I truly wanted to talk to Hitler directly. To me, it seemed logical that this dreaded Nazi leader would be able to see that he need not be afraid of us and would then leave us alone. I was certain I could convince him, that if he met face to face with a nice little Jewish girl who approached him politely and who was truthful to him, he would see the error of his ways. I was so certain that I could change the course of world events.

Oh, well. At least I was able to bring a smile back to Papa's face.

#

By spring 1940, my parents changed languages again. They often turned to their native Polish now, and I knew why. With every day's distressing news, Papa began making contingency plans for our family and he didn't want me to know them. He wasn't going to take any chances, I heard him say once. He knew the Germans.

Maman frequently wept when she thought no one was near. She and Papa still had close family ties in Poland.

#

My father talked a lot about how too many French people believed the *Ligne* Maginot would protect our country from invasion. He thought those people were all wrong. He said the *Ligne*'s fixed guns could not be turned if the enemy came from another direction. So, what good were they?

This logic did not become apparent to enough people until it was too late. Then, slowly, with what my father described as *insouciance*, the French government made institutional changes to a state of readiness for possible attack on Paris. Subway stations, department store basements, cellars of apartment buildings all became bomb shelters. An air raid alert and public protection plan were adopted and activated. Each neighborhood now had its local air-raid wardens and early warning procedures.

Our school implemented an air raid program and scheduled drills frequently. We were taught how to use our desks to protect our heads during an air attack. Almost daily we were drilled in the correct responses and procedures to be followed at home. Each of us was issued a personal gas mask and instructed in its use; we were also taught how to apply wet handkerchiefs over our noses and mouths as a substitute in the absence of masks, if needed.

All Parisians were ordered to cover their windows and exterior doorframes with heavy, double drapes. Blackout curfews were now strictly enforced. Special wardens patrolled the streets after dark, and citations were given if even a small stream of light penetrated the night from a window, doorway, or from a cigarette mindlessly drawn outdoors. The City of Light was now a city in darkness.

Even though Paris had prepared for possible air attacks, the first air raid was nevertheless a shock to all Parisians. No one had ever imagined that our beloved city would be bombed. But one day, sirens went off in some distant part of the city and all Paris froze.

From that moment, the frequency, intensity, and number of air raids increased. It became difficult to get a full night's sleep, so we began going to bed fully clothed in case we had to jump out of bed and run for shelter in the middle of the night.

When the night raids were not too close to our home, we turned out the lights and slipped in front of the thick air raid curtains to see what was happening outside. Sometimes, the sky was overcast and we only heard the oppressive drone of hundreds of bombers flying above. Nevertheless, Paris' powerful searchlights probed the cloud cover, crisscrossing the heavens over and over in a vain effort to pierce the clouds that gave protection to the enemy.

On other occasions, the clouds were thin. A searchlight beam found its mark and followed a tiny plane far above in the night sky. A second beam, then a third quickly joined the first two and our French *canons*, aiming at these crosshairs, began their noisy barrage. Billows of smoke from popping charges followed their missed target. But once in a while, an explosion lit up the sky more brilliantly than other times and I knew one less bomber would threaten us that night.

On a late Sunday, sirens began to wail with an urgency and intensity I had not heard before. With a chill, I immediately understood why. The sirens were those of our own neighborhood's air raid warning station; they were close and so loud they hurt my ears. We grabbed our gas masks (always near at hand) and scurried for our blankets, in case they might be needed to protect us from falling debris. Was this merely one of the frequent practice alerts or the real thing? But, as we had learned to do, we made our way down the stairs as quickly as we could.

Oh! There they were. The dreaded dive-bombers were, indeed, overhead.

The unmistakable characteristic rising whine of their engines in rapid descent told us with chilling certainty what the next sound would be.

(After all these years, this image still flashes back in my mind whenever I hear a plane in steep descent--and I am eight years-old again in 1940 Paris.)

Papa grabbed Eveline and me. With her under one arm and me hanging onto his other hand for dear life, we nearly flew down the remaining stairs of our apartment building and ran across the courtyard; Maman and the baby were at Papa's heels. By the time we reached the top step of our complex's basement shelter, we heard the chilling scream of the first bomb hurtling downward toward us. Hurling ourselves down the remaining basement steps, we reached the bottom just in time.

The explosion was deafening and much too close.

We all lunged for one another at the same time. After a heart-stopping moment and listening intently, Papa led us toward a clear space against the cellar's old but very solid and thick stone walls. As I had been taught to do, I quickly put on my gas mask.

How I despised that mask. I hated the sickeningly sweet smell of rubber that made me feel queasy; the forced, measured breathing to get needed air; the heavy weight that pulled my head forward; the tightness of the rubber mask and straps around my face and head; the hollow, muffled sound of my voice when I tried to speak. Above all, I hated my rising panic each time I put it on. But, although I felt trapped by this contraption, I knew I had no choice.

Since ours was an official neighborhood shelter, it was well stocked with food, water, first-aid supplies, emergency lights, blankets, and cots. I felt reasonably safe there. And I knew we could be there for several hours. I looked around at all the people sitting on the floor with their backs propped up against a wall and wondered if they were as frightened as I.

Then we heard it … the scream of the second bomb!

Silence fell. Everyone's eyes turned upward. Adults and children alike clutched at loved ones. Maman pressed Paulette to her breast, and Papa tightened his grip on my hand. The beating of my heart pounded in my ears. We all listened anxiously, fearful of what might come next.

As suddenly as it began, the scream stopped. My heart was in my mouth. I counted silently, one, … two, … KRAAAHH BOOOOMMM!

The building shook; fine dust came out of the mortared walls and filled the air; the basement's few bare hanging light bulbs went out for an instant and came on again in their now-swinging sockets. Children screamed and began to cry; some adults whimpered, others whispered prayers. I pressed closer to Papa. He put his arms around me and squeezed hard.

A new hush now settled over everyone. We all held our breaths. Overhead, tumult quickly followed. Male voices were shouting somewhere outside; from the courtyard above, we heard sounds of running feet. Almost immediately, the urgent *weehhh-wauhhh-weehhh-wauhhh* of the *pompiers'* trucks sounded, announcing the firemen's arrival. Others were soon heard to join them.

I cringed, fearing the worst. Oh, no! Where was the fire?

But we knew the rules. No one could go out until we were told it was safe to do so. The waiting seemed endless. It felt like hours passed before the "all clear" was sounded, and longer still before the air raid warden told us the raid was over and we could emerge from our underground shelter. Only then, would we know if it was our home that had been hit.

Finally, we were allowed to go up. Emergency vehicles and personnel were everywhere. We made our way up nervously through the crowd. My heart was in my mouth once more. Would our home be gone?

I held my breath, anxiously scanning the courtyard as we came out. *Is our building...?*

Ahh! What relief! Not this time. This time, we were spared. But, the top floor of the building next door was demolished.

#

Not surprisingly, I did not finish the school term that spring. Maman wanted me home all the time. There were air raids almost daily and I was so very frightened.

It was now late May 1940.

#

By mid-June, the fighting was all over. An armistice was requested by the French government and was signed in late June in order to save Paris. Our French military strategists had woefully overestimated the effectiveness of the Maginot defenses and underestimated the Germans' resourcefulness and strength.

#

On June 14, 1940, a Sunday, our family was called to the home of a family friend, a businessman across the street whose apartment overlooked the large *Place de la République.* By the time we arrived, several friends and their relatives had already gathered there. I was struck by the sorrow I saw and felt that day. The women and older children sobbed quietly. Most of the men, in their grief, joined in and wept openly at the sight that met their eyes outside. As French patriots, we felt a deep sense of loss for our beloved country. But there was another feeling in the room; a foreboding was intermingled with that sorrow because all of us in this room were Jews!

The streets below had been completely cleared. The formal arrival of the massive German army into Paris had begun. Thousands upon thousands of German troops, materiel-laden trucks, and tanks with guns at the ready were being paraded down the *Grands Boulevards.* Escorting them overhead were hundreds, if not thousands, of fighter planes and bombers droning ominously low. As far as my eyes could see, on the pavement below was a churning gray sea of swastikas and goose-stepping boots.

This disgustingly arrogant show of force was staged to humiliate and demoralize the French people. And it had its

planned effect. This year, there were no fireworks from the
Eiffel Tower to celebrate Bastille Day, no parties, no laughter,
no liberty--only the echo of thousands of marching boots to
augment our sorrow, our tears, and our fears.

#

A new French government was soon set up to replace the
one that had collapsed. Its official headquarters were in Vichy,
approximately two hundred miles south of Paris. To the chagrin
of some but to the satisfaction of others, there were many Nazi
sympathizers in this rightist Vichy government. [5]

During the first few months of the occupation, Vichy adopted
a position of full cooperation regarding its foreign-born Jews.
Vichy claimed this was a negotiated quid pro quo for leaving its
native-born Jewish citizens alone.

But this deal was not made out of a sense of humanitarianism or loyalty to its French Jews. Rather, it was out of self-
interest--given the important role the French-born Jews played
in the French economy. However, the Nazis were just as eager
as Vichy to have the country's economy stabilized as quickly as
possible. Therefore, they made certain major concessions at the
outset.

One of these was Vichy "autonomy" over a portion of France
euphemistically labeled the "Free Zone" by the Germans.
This zone, the southern third of France, started at the Swiss
border northeast of Lyons, and followed a westerly line above
Châteauroux north of the Loire River. It then turned south
toward the Pyrénées.

Other German concessions gave Vichy administrative control
and management of the infrastructure of France, the central hub
of which was of course, Paris. All main roads and rail lines
led to the French capital. But at the same time, the Germans

---

5 The pogroms of Jews in Eastern Europe resulted in thousands of persecuted Jews fleeing to France for safety in the 1930s. Right-wing sympathizers
in France looked upon them as a drain on the French economy.

demanded clear access to France; roads and rail lines had to be kept open for their priority use. To accomplish this, stringent travel restrictions were placed on French citizens. Administered and enforced by Vichy, these restrictions were under strict policy direction of the Germans.

Now, in order to track the movement of people, travel permits were required for either exit from, or entry into Paris. Due to the population drain from the capital immediately following the occupation of Paris, and the inevitable underground backlash that quickly followed, these permits became nearly impossible to obtain--especially for Jews.

#

Long before the Germans ever reached Paris, my father's contingency plans for our family's departure from Paris had been checked and rechecked. A natural survivor, his instincts were uncanny. Within hours following the arrival of the German army and before they had closed all the roads out of the City, his plans were in place to leave Paris. He was to leave by car first; the rest of our little family would follow not too long after by train. He felt we stood a better chance of getting out successfully if we split up and did not leave Paris together.

Besides, Papa had a lot of bundles and valuables he needed to take with him. There was merchandise that could later be sold for income, as well as important family documents and business dossiers. He also took family clothing, jewels, and, most important, he took cash.

There was no other way to get anything out of Paris at this time. The postal system was censored and unreliable, and other shipping systems were unavailable to the ordinary citizen. Papa did not know how long we would be away from Paris, but just in case, he was prepared for a long siege. He and a friend joined forces and devised a plan for the relocation of their families.

The two men decided to leave together. By so doing, they could relieve each other driving as well as bring their precious cargoes along. The southern route that Papa had to take was very dangerous. The Germans had already closed most of the major roads out of Paris in an effort to stanch the hemorrhage of the city's population. And, to keep these roads clear for the German war machine, surgical air strikes over them were frequent in the earliest days of the occupation.

Since Papa was a licensed manufacturer and government contractor, he had an authorized pre-war commercial travel license on record, and his need to travel was not challenged. His foreign birth gave him some anxious moments though--and he would probably not be able to return safely. But he nevertheless succeeded in obtaining his travel documents promptly.

Before he left, Papa admonished Maman, "You must not do anything that looks unusual. You must not raise the suspicion of neighbors or strangers that you're leaving Paris for good or you may be arrested. Take only small bags that you can carry by hand. *Il ne faut rien dire à personne,* say nothing to anyone."

Neighbors had often seen Papa leave with large packages when he called on customers in the provinces. It would appear normal for him to have such big bundles of "merchandise" with him when he left.

Whereas, he reasoned, if Maman took the children with more than is needed for a short summer vacation, it would be noticed. And if the authorities were notified of such unusual behavior on our part, they might not allow us to leave. Maman spoke perfect French with no accent, and neither she nor the children "looked" Jewish, so he felt we would be all right if we did nothing to alert neighbors or to attract the attention of the Vichy authorities. He would leave in the pre-dawn hours, Papa said, before Paris stirred, and be gone before anyone awoke.

It all happened so quickly. That's how it came to be that I woke up one morning shortly after the Germans marched into Paris, and found out that Papa was gone. All Maman would say was that he would be away for awhile this time, but we would see him soon. It sounded so indefinite; I missed him already.

In the meantime, she said we should go about our normal activities. For her, it included selling merchandise at the *Marché St. Ouen*, the big Saturday regional market where you could buy anything that qualified as consumer goods. This was something she had already been doing to generate extra income. Now, she needed to convert all the remaining merchandise into cash before we left. I sensed a new urgency in her behavior; with Papa gone, it made me feel even more anxious.

Thus came about the first of several wrenching family separations.

#

It didn't take long before the foreign-born Jews of France were treated like hunted animals by Vichy. Maman had already begun to think and behave accordingly. She kept what she knew to herself and didn't tell me anything sensitive so that I would not innocently give away information that might betray escape plans, but I had overheard enough of my parents' conversations to have a sense of what was to come. Being the curious nearly nine-year-old I was, I sometimes listened at closed doors, and I knew that their secrets must also be my secrets. I had taken the first step on my way to maturity and to being a child survivor: learning as much as I could, and keeping my mouth shut.

On the eve of our own departure some time in July, Maman asked me to sit down for a serious talk following an unusually early dinner. I was all ears. Serious talks always made me feel grown-up.

"Jacqueline, *Chérie.*" Hmm, no nickname this time, I thought. This must, indeed, be something serious.

"Jacqueline, I want you to listen carefully. Tomorrow morning, we will all leave here very, very early. It will still be dark outside…"

"Are we going to the beach for vacation?" I interrupted eagerly.

"*Non, mon chou.* Not to the beach. But we will be going on a train for a sort of vacation."

She went on to say that contrary to what I had always done in the past when we went on our usual family vacations, I was not to take any of my things along. She would pack all that I would need.

"Now, I have a most important job for you that will help me to be a good Maman for all three of you during this trip."

My chest swelled as I listened. The next morning, I was to watch over my sister, Eveline, until we reached the train. She emphasized that I was to hold onto my little sister's hand and not let go no matter what. What a grown-up job!

That wasn't all. I would have my very own satchel to carry in my other hand; and I was to stay very, very close to her at all times. There would be a lot of people everywhere at the station and it would be easy to get separated.

Furthermore, I was not to speak to anyone and I was to keep my eyes down if anyone did come near us. She especially stressed that I was not to look directly at any soldiers or policemen. Something in her voice found its mark in my soul; I knew I must do exactly as she asked.

"*Tu as compris, Chérie?* Is that understood, Darling?" She said in her most serious voice. "Now go to bed."

"*Oui, Maman.*" I answered quietly in my own solemn voice, my chest again swelling with pride at the thought of having been given such grown-up responsibilities: my little three-year-old sister, and baggage too!

But, I asked myself, why should I not look at people? That was a strange thing that Maman had asked of me. Of course I would do as I was told. She always knew the right thing to do, I reminded myself. I had to admit I had felt some anxiety at her words. So, I decided that I would not let Maman down. I could tell something important was happening, and I had a significant part in it.

I knew. Deep down, I sensed it. Irreparably, the only world I had ever known had begun to crumble. In the pit of my stomach, the beginnings of fear began to nudge, a kind of fear I had never experienced before, one that sharpens all the senses. It was to grow inside of me, and become my constant companion for the three years that followed.

My dark world of survival had begun.

CHAPTER VI

Adieu, Paris!

Dawn had not yet risen when we left our elegant Paris apartment and all the lovely things with which Maman and Papa had lovingly furnished it. Though I did not know it at the time, never again would I see these possessions so integral to the few precious years I call my true childhood. The family treasures that made up our home were placed under provisional administration and expropriated by the Vichy authorities some time after our departure from Paris. The things I had grown to cherish are now images that irrationally continue to haunt my memory.

I was not quite nine years of age on that chilly pre-dawn in the summer of 1940. Eveline was barely three, and Paulette, still nursing and wearing night diapers, was just about to turn two.

Our immediate destination was the *Gare d'Orléans/ Austerlitz,* the railroad station whose trains serve south-central France. During peacetime, we often took its fast, comfortable passenger trains when we went off on one of our family's carefree month-long August vacations. Today, however, there was neither speed nor comfort and, as I soon learned, it was no carefree family vacation.

Instead of dressing in light summer clothing, we all wore several layers of what were relatively warm clothes for a summer trip. Maman had planned it that way. The reason was twofold. First, we had to have our hands free for the little ones. So, to keep baggage light, Maman had us wear our changes of clothes instead of carrying them. Second, and more important, the linings and shoulder pads of our jackets and coats were effective places to hide valuables. Maman had spent many hours ripping seams open and pulling out stuffing from shoulder pads and linings, to make room for cash and jewelry; then, she stitched them closed once more. When she had finished and had pressed our garments, it was virtually impossible to find any signs of alteration or of the valuables that were hidden from view. The clothes we wore were drab and dark in color. Maman deliberately avoided dressing any of us in our more stylish, expensive outfits. Our general appearance was probably very similar to that of provincial travelers who circulated constantly throughout Paris on bartering business in the nation's large central markets.

"We must blend into the crowd and not attract attention," Maman had said, putting back a colorful top I wanted to wear. She had planned everything carefully.

When we arrived at the station, people were waiting or milling about everywhere. So many wanted to leave Paris. I was awed and frightened. I had never seen this many human beings in one place before, even at the circus. Some were standing; others were sitting on hurriedly packed belongings. Many, especially children and old people, were sprawled asleep on the ground, their heads resting on makeshift pillows of clothing bundles. Despite the early hour, the station was noisy--and the stench of unwashed bodies made my nostrils twitch. People had obviously been waiting there a long time.

No trains were running--at least not for ordinary French citizens. The entire elegant first and second-class, as well as the not-so-elegant third and fourth-class, passenger trains had been commandeered by the Germans. Refreshment concessions were closed. Food had become scarce; everything that came in from the provinces was immediately shipped to the German army. The little that remained for French consumers was snapped up in minutes from depleted market shelves except, of course, food bound for an already burgeoning black market.

Maman pressed her way along, maneuvering us through the throngs of shouting, gesticulating men and women. She seemed to know where she had to go and stopped to speak to several harried railway attendants. I watched her discreetly slip something into their hands, and somehow, miraculously, we were unobtrusively directed through the frenzied crowds. As we made our way toward the track area, the sounds of humanity that had echoed off the high ceilings of the station's great hall began to dim. The stillness of the night outside was almost ominous. We were now heading in the direction of the freight yards. Many boxcars were filled with sleeping people. Maman said she was looking for a car with enough space to accommodate all of us comfortably.

We walked for what seemed hours to me. The passenger platforms were soon behind us, then the structures of the station complex. Still, we walked. We passed the loading docks of the freight area, and we headed toward the stockyards. By now, the sky had taken on a gray hue. I held Eveline tightly by the hand as Maman had instructed me to do the night before. Every once in a while, I had to carry Paulette for a short time while Maman picked up Eveline who was now very tired. We stopped often to rest. The girls were heavy and I was afraid of dropping my precious load. There were no lights out here. It was still too dark to see clearly, so we picked our way slowly over the gravel and railway ties. We peered into each crowded boxcar looking for available space as we went. I tried not to let Maman see that I was getting tired myself. She kept saying how brave she thought I was. I didn't want to disappoint her.

At some point, she got help from a railway employee who said he would show us where there were some empty cars. His swinging lantern lit our way so I could see better now, and he helped us carry the children so we moved faster too. By this time, I was certain that we were going to walk all the way to our destination--wherever that might be.

I had no sense of distance but it felt to my tired legs as though we must have covered several kilometers out of the city itself. By the time we reached the covered cattle cars, dawn

had arrived. At least now, we could see our way better. Maman
checked each car carefully. Many of them were already filled.
Finally, she looked into one and said,

"*Voilà! Enfin.*" This is it!

It was an old car on a track away from the main ones and not
presently attached to either of the cars closest to it. It had been
recently put back into circulation. Its top was solid but the sides
consisted of roughly hewn boards stacked on their edges, one on
top of another horizontally, and were kept in place by pairs of
heavy metal posts at each corner. Except for a little straw strewn
here and there, the car was otherwise totally empty and its big
open sliding doors seemed to say,

"I've been waiting for you. Hurry up, get in before someone
else comes."

The yard attendant helped me up. Maman thanked him
in her most elegant French manner, giving him one of her
beautiful, coquettish smiles--along with a nice tip--and he left
after promising to bring some more straw. I was too tired to ask
her what she planned to do with it.

We were now alone. A familiar smell teased my nostrils
in the windowless car. It was reminiscent of the barn at the
wet nurse's farm and scenes from the couple of summers I had
spent there briefly flashed across my mind. But, despite the
unmistakable odor of cow dung, the car still appeared relatively
clean. Maman carefully selected just the right place for us, in the
far right corner of the car, diagonally across from the door. The
location seemed important to her. It had two walls for support,
shelter from the front entrance in case rain should come, and a
view through the open doors so we could see what was going on
outside.

Eveline had cried a lot from fatigue despite the small sedating
potion she had been given. But, mercifully, Paulette--whose
cries were normally irritatingly loud--had slept most of the time
in the sling Maman had fashioned for herself.

What was obviously on Maman's mind now was to have us catch up on our sleep, so she went about making us as comfortable as she could. She gathered what straw there was on the floor and created a soft pad for Eveline and me. The carpetbags she had carried, she placed against the car wall to serve as pillows, and then she instructed me, *"Couche-toi au coin et mets Eveline à ta droite."* (Lie down in the corner and put Eveline on your right.). Paulette came next with Maman seated on Paulette's right. This family line-up remained in place for all the days that followed, with me in my corner securing one end and Maman guarding the other.

Since a bit of pre-dawn chill was still in the air, Maman covered us with her coat, and tucked us in the best she could. Finally, placing herself between her children and the rest of the car, she settled down in her own place and prepared to breast-feed her baby.

While Paulette suckled hungrily, Maman began to sing to us her old, comforting lullaby that we loved so much. We knew it by heart.

"Hai-lo, lo-lo, lo-lo, lo-lo, Eveline va faire ... son p'ti-it ... do-do..."

Soon, thumb in mouth, Eveline's eyes began to close. And, not too long after, I too, fell into a deep exhausted sleep.

I have no sense of how long I slept. When I awoke, I quickly noted that our "train" had not moved out of the stockyards, and we were no longer alone. Several other people had come into the car, perhaps a dozen or so. And they looked like they were settling in for a long stay too. There was a lot of jockeying for territory and comfort. Maman had been wise to bring us so early.

It was probably now well into the afternoon. Three bales of straw had been added to our corner. Two were stacked on Maman's right side so as to provide her with a little "privacy," and one was at my feet. This created somewhat of an enclosure for our family, perhaps three feet deep by five feet long. A few other bales were stacked here and there and more straw now covered the car floor.

Magically, a small porcelain enamel wash basin and a bottle of water had appeared in our little corner, as well as a small chamber pot with a piece of cardboard as a makeshift lid to cover it. Maman had truly thought of everything.

I was ravenous. As though she read my mind, from one of her packages, she pulled out raisins, biscuits, dark chocolate, canned milk and the Lu Lu shortbread cookies that I loved. Her stores also included bottled water and canned *pâté*, sardines, hard cheese, and dry salami--no fresh vegetables or fruit. Except for an occasional and exorbitantly priced black-market purchase, we had not been able to buy fresh produce since the Germans had occupied Paris a few weeks earlier.

While she handed us our food portions, I noticed other tin boxes in Maman's bag. They made good, airtight, varmint-proof storage containers for perishables like salami, cheese and cookies. She had obviously planned for a long trip. I didn't understand why. For all of our other summer trips, picnic lunches were all we brought. Our destination was always reached the same day. France is not such a large country and most trips could be completed in one day.

This time, we had a cup and two spoons. For our personal *toilette*, we all shared a wash-mitt and small towel. Maman had also brought a piece of soap and a diaper rag. While I savored my cheese, I marveled at all she brought. Having weighed benefits against extra baggage, she brought only the most vital items. With Paulette still in night diapers, she had to have soap. Despite these provisions, it was still nearly impossible to maintain any semblance of true hygiene.

As I munched contentedly, daylight turned to dusk. Soon, several little lights went on in the car. Some people had brought a few candles and matches with them. How comforting those lights were. But how dangerous with all that straw! However, I did not think of things like that then.

Food appeared mysteriously here and there when hunger could no longer be ignored. One or two bottles of table wine furtively sought thirsty lips, and then even more surreptitiously returned to secret hiding places. Most people had brought provisions. A few did not have anything for warmth in the cold of night; so they curled up in the fetal position or pressed against one another to maximize the benefits of body heat. After awhile, I became aware that a few people had put aside their culturally ingrained tendency toward discretion and social restraint with strangers, and were quietly talking to each other, perhaps exchanging information.

Maman did not encourage verbal exchanges with others in the car. She believed the less said, the better. Leaning over, she whispered to me that I was to stay in my corner, not speak to anyone, and to watch our belongings carefully. Softly, she reminded me that if anyone--especially a soldier or uniformed guard--came toward our corner of the car, I was to avoid making any eye contact with him.

"Slide down onto the floor and hide behind your bale of straw if someone approaches you."

"Why, Maman?" I whispered in return.

She leaned over further, "Because some German soldiers may come to see if there are any Jews here." She answered between nearly closed lips so that others in the car would not hear that we were Jews.

"What will they do if they find us?" I queried.

"I don't know *Chérie*. But I don't want to take any chances on being taken off this train."

"Is this a real train? Will it leave soon?" I pressed further, wanting desperately to be on our way already and not understanding why we had not yet departed.

She tried her best to explain, that she had been told the train would leave soon, but there was some delay. She didn't know why.

"So, please don't ask anymore, *Chérie.*"

I could sense her concern, her worry, her fear--and they became mine as well.

We talked quietly for a while as she prepared the girls for sleep. She cleaned Paulette's little behind with the soap and the small rag she had brought for that purpose, and put a clean diaper on her. Once powdered and diapered, Paulette sat playing contentedly with the straw while Maman attended to Eveline who was sitting on the chamber pot--something she seemed to like doing a lot. I put a scratch on the board above my head to mark the end of the day. And a routine began to emerge for the long evenings that were to follow.

Next morning, still on the same track in Paris, more people came into our car--I lost count. A railway attendant came to look in as if to see if we were all there, and told us a soldier would be coming soon. Just a routine check, he said.

"*Oh, Pardon, Monsieur!*" Maman called out and got up to ask him something. He responded and nodded his head, his hands in constant motion. When she returned to our corner, she picked up the chamber pot; by this time, it had become fetid and full to the brim. Slowly, carefully, she lifted it; with the skill of a ballet dancer, she made her way to the door without spilling one drop. She would not be gone long, she said. She was merely going to empty her malodorous vessel and be right back.

True to her word, she was back a short while later and returned the now empty chamber pot to its usual corner. She then picked up the empty water bottle and told me that she would be gone a little longer this time. She had to find drinking water.

"*Fais attention, Jacqueline!*" she said. "Watch our things. And, don't let your sisters wander out of this corner."

I did not like it one bit when she left us. I got such a tight feeling in the pit of my stomach. With each passing minute, my heart beat faster and my mouth became dry while my anxiety increased.

When will Maman come back? What if she never comes back? What if the train leaves before she returns? What will become of me? How will Papa find us? Will someone try to steal our food? Or, steal my little sisters? Maybe it will be one of the men on this car; one of the mean-looking unshaven ones that just arrived today! My thoughts ran pell-mell over the possibilities.

I looked around fearfully to see who might be watching, waiting. Each face seemed more threatening to me than the one before. I clutched my sisters close to me, sang a nervous round of *Frères Jacques* and pressed further and further into my corner.

Suddenly, there she was! Maman had just appeared within the framed daylight of the open doors. An unbelievable wave of relief and joy washed over me. Tears welled up in my eyes. How comforting it was to see her. She put her two bottles of water, now full, on the floor of the car and eased herself up. I relaxed my grip on my sisters and ran to her, jumping over the legs of people as I went, and threw my arms around her sobbing.

"Oh, Maman, Maman! I was so afraid. I thought you were never coming back."

"I know, *Chérie.* I know." Pressing me to her bosom, she caressed me lovingly. "Jacqueline, *mon chou,* I would never leave you and your sisters."

These were words she had said several times before, but they were still not enough to allay my fears whenever she left us even for a moment. I was now old enough to have some appreciation of how threatening the world around me could be and how truly helpless I was in it.

I gave Maman a hand carrying the bottles over to our corner and sat back down. With the little bar of soap and the small towel that was already beginning to turn gray from use, we then began our *toilette.*

For now, at least, I was safe.

\#

"Achtung!" a male voice shouted.

I froze. There, framed in the doorway and brandishing a rifle in front of him was the German soldier we had been told about the day before. We were still in Paris, on the same track, in the same rail stockyard. Suddenly remembering Maman's instructions about not making eye contact with soldiers, I quickly put my head down and shrank into my corner. Eveline's hand found its way into mine and I put my arm around my little sister. Maman slid down behind the bale of straw and inched close to me. She pulled Paulette towards her and squeezed her to her bosom. The sudden pressure made the baby cry. But in an instant, Maman had pulled out one of her breasts and pushed it into the toddler's mouth. The crying ceased as suddenly as it started. I looked at Paulette. Maman was holding the toddler's head firmly against her breast; I found myself wondering how the baby could breathe.

A hush settled over our now overcrowded cattle car. People were bunched together. There was barely enough space for one's feet. That was probably a good thing for us. With thirty to forty people in the car, we four were not likely to be noticed too readily.

I was terrified. Yet, curiosity got the better of me. Keeping my head down, I rolled my eyes up as far as they would go. Now, I could just barely see what was going on. It was still very early in the morning and most people in the car were either still lying down or sitting.

The German officer stood, legs apart, his polished black boots and gun belt reflected the morning light. Coldly, deliberately threatening, he scanned the crowd. Is he looking for something or someone, I wondered? In front of him, his rifle was poised for instant action. Now, it slowly swept over the crowd, shouting its terrifying soundless warning. For a brief moment, as it scanned toward my corner, it stopped and seemed to point at me. Startled, my eyes popped fully open and I looked up at the soldier's face. *Oh, oh! Did he just look at me?* I immediately shut my eyes tight and shrank further down behind my bale of straw.

The silence in the car was deafening. No one spoke. No one moved.

Suddenly, he spat out some words in German. To my young ears, it sounded as though he had something caught in his throat that he was trying to expel at the same time that he was asking a question. Maman caught her breath. (She was fluent in German.)

I could tell she was terribly frightened. I began to whimper and tremble. Tears filled my eyes. If my maman--who was a tower of strength and always knew what to do--was frightened, what hope was there? *This is it,* I thought. *We are doomed. Any minute now, the German soldier will point his gun at us and ... that will be the end. We will never see Papa again.*

Instead, Maman furtively sought my hand and squeezed it so tight it hurt. But it was just what I needed to stop shaking.

Then, as suddenly as he had appeared, the soldier stepped back, jumped off the train car and was gone.

As one, Maman and I lunged for each other, clutching, sobbing, and hugging so tight that I could barely breathe. But I didn't mind at all.

#

After the German soldier left, nothing else happened. The day wore on. Time dragged horribly with nothing to do but try to keep Eveline from wandering off into someone else's space. I had one toy, my string game. This simple loop of string that was slipped onto, and held by, the fingers of each hand was a favorite of mine. When the loop was pulled taught, it formed two parallels that challenged the opponent. The objective was to lift the loop off your opponent's hand by creating different intricate patterns from the two parallels. Many possibilities existed. You first had to lift one side with certain fingers of one hand, and then lift the other side with the fingers of the other hand before sliding the entire loop off the opponent's hand. Hours could be spent on the game. The last player who was able to create a pattern was the winner.

Eveline was too young to play this game with me so all I could do was try to weave new patterns alone. I pretended I had a partner and contorted my hands and arms in a vain effort to pull through a new pattern while I tried to hold onto the old one. This effort was more of a challenge than the actual game.

Twilight finally came.

That night, I did not sleep well. The soldier had frightened me terribly, and I had developed a rash that itched a lot. In addition, the thunderous snores of the many noses close by were as deafening as a brass marching band in a tunnel. To make matters worse, the stink of unwashed bodies and human waste around me was beginning to make me feel queasy. I tossed and turned on my bed of straw until finally, exhausted from scratching and worrying over what the next day would bring, I fell into fitful sleep.

#

Meals became makeshift affairs. The first day, we had three meals. But Maman soon changed the meal schedule to twice a day when she realized that we might have to make our provisions last for quite a while. Though we ate hungrily at first, as our selection dwindled, so did our enthusiasm for what remained. The raisins were finished within the first couple of days. The biscuits were gone, the shortbreads were gone, and the cheese was gone. We were now pretty much on a diet of salami and sardines--not my favorites at the age of almost nine. However, there was still some hard chocolate that Maman carefully rationed for special treats. She was increasingly reluctant to use it up. She explained that she did not want to take the chance of leaving us alone for long periods to look for food, in case the train should leave. So, she managed with the little bit we had.

The rail car was still where we first saw it on its tracks in the Paris yard three mornings earlier, or was it four? Though I tried very hard to keep track of the days--perhaps because I so much wanted to see Papa again, or perhaps to simply have something to do--it was difficult to distinguish one day from another.

#

This particular morning was overcast and humid. It was characteristic of Paris summer weather with rain not far off and with it, welcome relief. But, meanwhile, the air in the car was oppressively heavy and malodorous. Little trips to the door for a breath of fresh air did not help me.

"I don't feel good, Maman." I whimpered as I rolled over to face her.

"What is it, *Chérie?*"

She looked down at me tenderly with concern in her eyes and put her hand to my forehead to assess my temperature. Apparently, she was satisfied. I was too uncomfortable to wonder how she could take my temperature without a thermometer like she always did at home.

A flash of lightening brightened the heavens and, for an instant, the dark interior of the car was flooded with light. Within seconds, the first clap of thunder came crashing around us. The storm, in all its fury, had arrived. Soon, the plop-plop of heavy drops of water resonated throughout the car. Then in a rush, sheets of water came thundering down. Though nearly deafening, it was somehow comforting, and the air was thankfully refreshed; a cool breeze soon swept through the car, cleansing our nostrils and cooling our skin.

"My stomach hurts." I said plaintively.

For the remainder of the day, I frequently got up to sit on the chamber pot. Poor Maman. She had to take the foul thing out so many times that day, in the pouring rain too.

But, the rain was nevertheless a blessing--in more ways than one. We needed water so badly, for washing as well as for drinking.

It rained such a long time that day that Maman was able to collect rainwater in the washbasin. She stood at the edge of the doorway and held the basin out as far as she could; it was raining so hard that the little basin filled up quickly. Then, to avoid spilling her precious load, she carefully picked her way back to us over the clutter of knees and feet that lay between the car door and our corner. The dirty water was carried back in the same manner to be tossed out.

She repeated this routine many times, and we were finally able to wash all over. She even managed to rinse out diapers, as well as some of our clothes, and drape them over the bales of straw to dry.

Maman insisted on washing our hair too. Poor Eveline got soap in her eyes and wouldn't stop crying for a long time. While Maman was combing out her hair, she suddenly let out a sound of such repugnance that I could only imagine she had seen a worm or, even worse, a dead mouse. It was neither.

"Aaarrghh!" She recoiled, horrified.

Quickly, she examined my own head. To her dismay, she found what she'd feared. Lice!

For the better part of the afternoon, she attempted to remove as many of the little bloodsucking beasts from our heads as she could find. She showed me how to remove them myself whenever I felt the characteristic tickling, stinging sensation on my own scalp that soon became all too familiar.

This delousing, also, became part of our daily routine now. How I hated those little beasts.

#

Toward the end of the week, another railway employee paid us a visit. He told us our departure had been delayed because "*Les Boches,*" (the Nazi 'pigs') had taken over every rail line out of Paris. He said they had commandeered all the locomotives as well as most of the boxcars. But he did say that one locomotive had finally been released to the French railway company. Our car was soon going to be coupled to others and we would, at last, truly be part of a train. No, he could not tell us exactly when we would be on our way, as the Germans had not yet given them final clearance. Meantime, he told us to prepare for sudden lurching when the coupling began. Then, he closed and latched the doors.

It became almost pitch black inside. Horizontal slits of light came through between some of the boards. For the next few hours, these narrow cracks were our only source of light and air. The waiting seemed interminable. Hours felt like days. There were occasional screeches of rail brakes somewhere behind us, but none of the lurching we had been told to expect. We were still exactly where we'd started, how many days ago?

Suddenly, just as I began to wonder if the railway people had totally forgotten us, there it was! A loud screech was heard, then a thump, and the long awaited lurch, more screeching, several more lurches forward. Then, the sounds of clanging chains and, the final clunks of heavy metal pins reached us. At long last, we were coupled to something.

Boisterous shouts of joy came from everyone in our car. This was the most excitement we'd had since our arrival. My heart was pounding from the anticipation of seeing Papa soon. Could it be true? We were going to leave at last. I looked over at Maman. She had one of her big, radiant smiles on her face. She was so beautiful, my Maman.

Now, since we expected to head out of Paris shortly after the coupling of the cars was done, the waiting became most difficult. We had allowed ourselves to become giddy at the prospect of soon being delivered from this stench.

But, hours passed and no further movement occurred. With day's end came total darkness. Since we had no light and couldn't move around, our only option was try to sleep. Unfortunately, I itched so badly that sleep eluded me for a long time. When sleep finally did come, it was again a fitful one.

I was startled out of this restless sleep by sharp, loud pounding against the sides and doors of our car. Equally loud and harsh commands were shouted in German at the same time. Then our doors were thrown open. The sky had just barely begun to lighten with the chilly dawn of a new day. A German soldier climbed into the car, shouting at people by the door. He shoved them out of his way with his rifle butt and kicked them with his boots. Someone outside put a lantern into the car so it was now possible to make out faces. The soldier, nevertheless, pulled out a flashlight and, with its bright beam piercing the darkness, scrutinized each face in turn. He stood above us, a threatening presence even to those of us who were crouched hidden in the shadows. Suddenly, he ordered one man, then another, to get out. And he was gone. [6]

The doors closed once more. Within a short time, we heard the long-awaited departure call from the yard up and down the track. A slight jerking followed as the cars adjusted, then, the squealing of metal against metal as wheels began turning and, incredibly, our train eased forward.

Enfin! Finally! Thank God. Slowly, with many stops and starts, it inched its way out of Paris. Thus, many days after we originally boarded, our train was at last on its way towards its southern destination.

---

6 I learned years later that an active underground effort had already begun to inflict serious damage to German supply and materiel convoys. Suspected members were picked up frequently for interrogation and possible internment.

CHAPTER VII

Heading South, at Last!

In the first few days that followed, there were frequent and extended stops, presumably to allow the passage of higher priority rail traffic. German troops were westbound from Germany for occupation assignments in France, and eastbound trains were filled with French food and goods for Germany's consumption. These non-stop trains continually caused us to be pulled off the main lines.

Tracks were shifted, engines needed scarce fuel or water, clearances had to be obtained from uncooperative or arbitrary bureaucrats, and inspections of cars and documents were continually conducted. A growing underground movement, disruptive to Berlin's plans and to Vichy's expected enforcement of them, had to be controlled; this was their highest priority. Therefore, all passenger-filled cattle rail cars were subjected to numerous inspections at nearly every stop before they could gain clearance to proceed.

We progressed at a snail's pace. Most of the time, the doors of our car were kept closed whether we were moving or not. As we inched farther south, the air outside became increasingly warm and, without windows, the interior felt like an oven. People's food and water supplies were nearly gone by this time. Everyone was listless, and unnecessary effort was avoided. Moving about was futile anyway; where could we have gone?

Our own initial meager supply of water was depleted after the second day out. Even if we had had extra water with which to wash, we had run out of soap and our one towel was filthier than we. Our food supply now consisted of half a salami. Maman's face was drawn. I doubt that she had been sleeping a great deal; she certainly was not eating much.

We were down to one meal per day. That meal became a ritual. I think Maman deliberately stretched it out as long as she could, as much to help pass the time as to make it appear that we had more food than we actually ate. She announced mealtime with great fanfare and enthusiasm. Making sure we were all seated in a little circle, she then, with a flourish, took out the paring knife she had brought and slowly, with surgical precision, she sliced the thinnest of slices for each of us. We watched longingly for this slice of dry salami that had become our only sustenance. I was ready to wolf down my portion immediately but Maman discouraged it.

"Suck on it for a while first, *Chérie.*" She instructed with parental firmness.

"*Oui, Maman.*"

"Bite off only small pieces, then chew them slowly, Jacqueline."

And, with another dramatic flourish, she shaved off another paper-thin slice of the tasty salami. I don't recall that she, herself, ate.

She always gave us the choicest food--even before The War--and selflessly served herself only from what was left. This was so characteristic of Maman. In our present situation, she probably went hungry most days so that we would have as much as she could possibly give us.

Chubby little Paulette did not look quite so chubby anymore, and she cried almost all the time she was awake. She had always been a restless, crying baby. Maman could not hold her in her arms for very long anymore because the toddler would hungrily reach for a breast that no longer satisfied her and would sometimes bite it in her fierce quest for food.

Eveline, who was ordinarily quiet and undemanding, cried too. The poor little thing was hungry. She was so much thinner now. And she had those awful draining sores on her arms and legs, just like the ones I had, but on her small body, they looked much bigger.

In addition, she was covered all over, as I was, with the same scabby rash that had been driving me to distraction. However, I could resist scratching sometimes, "to set the example," as I was told to do. But Eveline could not help herself. So, Maman wrapped her little hands with strips of handkerchief that she had torn up for that purpose in order to keep the child from scratching herself raw.

For nearly two days, we were truly miserable. It was too hot, we had no water, practically no food, and we itched constantly.

One day, despite the heat, I began to have chills and felt lightheaded. I had no energy to move at all; and I vomited what little food I had in my stomach. Maman was frantic. She broke down and cried to God and to anyone around us who would listen, about how she simply had to get water and food for her babies. To the others in the car she pleaded, wouldn't everybody please try to attract attention when the train stopped next so that the railroad attendant would come to unlatch the door? Poor Maman. There was more despair in her voice than I had ever heard.

An hour or so later, as if the locomotive's engineer himself had heard her, the train came to a stop. It was, in fact a scheduled stop at a little town not too far from Paris. Maman immediately began to pound on the car door and yell at the top of her voice. She was as close to hysteria as I had ever seen her. Then, perhaps because she was so distraught, she must have touched the hearts of others in the car. One by one, their own ferment rising to meet hers, they joined Maman pounding and shouting with her. The entire car reverberated until their clamor became a crescendo of wild outrage.

"*Salops!*" "Dirty pigs! Open the door. It's urgent!" they shouted for the world to hear. It was apparent that they too had reached the end of their patience. When aroused, the French can be formidable. The insufferable treatment we were all getting brought out their choicest epithets. Maman had truly rallied the support of our fellow travelers. Another French revolution was in the making.

Finally, the door slid open. Some of the people in our car had apparently reached their destination and got off. Although the station attendant had undoubtedly been given that information when they first boarded, I gave the credit for getting the door open to Maman's unmatched courage. Everyone in our car was standing now. Most people eagerly got off to look around and exercise their legs.

A-a-h-h. Fresh air. What a sweet, clean, blessed smell came into the car. That first long, invigorating breath was pure joy. Now, bright sunlight poured in. In fact, it was too bright for us at first. We had been in the dark so long that our blinking eyes did not adjust quickly anymore.

After a short time, however, the optical shock wore off. I could again see what was going on. Maman had naturally been among the first people to jump off the car when the doors opened. I could see her now, having an animated conversation with someone outside all the while gesticulating towards us. She looked determined. While she talked, a number of passengers returned, picked up their baggage and left. Thankfully, no new ones boarded. That meant more space for all of us.

Oh, thank you, thank you. There is a God after all, I thought.

Finally, it looked as though Maman had resolved something. She left the car with the empty water bottles under her arm, and brought them back full a short time later. She had apparently found potable water at the station house. What joy! Something as simple as water made my heart beat faster. Cautioning me not to gulp, Maman gave me the first drink. It was a lingering, luscious swallow. I felt the energy flow through my body instantly.

As it turned out, we were going to be at this stop for a time. Maman told me to lie down and rest while she took Paulette with her in search of food.

Though I still felt listless, I nevertheless wished hard and prayed to our Jewish God, as I had heard *Grandmère* do, that Maman would find lots of good things for us to eat. But, a short time later, she returned to say that the shops were closed; she was unable to find much. My heart sank.

But, she must have bargained with a local resident or shopkeeper, who probably took pity on the baby Maman had in her arms. She did bring back a little bread and cheese, as well as more water. That night, we ate better than we had for several days.

The train left the little station not long after Maman returned. Someone must have convinced the train attendant not to latch the doors from outside because they remained partly open as the train slowly pulled out. Oh, how happy I was to see the sky, the clouds, and the countryside going by through the door opening.

Thanks to those passengers who left earlier, there was more space. We were now more comfortable. We could stand up and walk a bit. One of the men in the car stood watch at the door to make sure that none of us came too close and fell out by accident. However, it is doubtful that anyone could have been hurt much by falling out of such a slow-moving train.

It stopped and started continually. We were heading into the open countryside, and there were many short stops. Maman took advantage of every opportunity to go in search of food. Since we were now moving through farmland, fresh food could be had for a price.

Once in a while, the train stopped long enough for Maman to go into a village. But she never took us with her; we would have slowed her down. We all three looked so awful that people might have thought we were carrying some kind of exotic disease-- which was probably not far from the truth. So, although our food supply remained scanty, we were less hungry than we had been earlier. As an added bonus, Maman was also somehow able to refill our water bottles regularly.

Before long, the summer heat of central France was upon us. At times, it became unbearably hot in our still crowded car. I nevertheless began to feel better now that I had food and water. For diversion, I treated myself to little strolls in the car and went exploring, picking my way gingerly among the many legs and feet. I smiled at a few people I had come to know and they smiled back. Sometimes we chatted briefly. My favorite pastime was to stand by the door to watch the summer landscape slowly go by. I remember thinking that, were I outside, I could probably walk as fast as the train moved.

One morning the train stopped altogether and did not start up again. We had arrived at the town of Vierzon. The stationmaster shouted that everyone was to remain in the cars; the end of the occupied zone had been reached.

German patrols were going through all the cars scrutinizing each passenger's travel documents. For some reason, and despite Maman's *"Laissez-passer aller et retour"* permit that authorized the bearer to leave and reenter the occupied zone, we were directed off the train along with several other people. Maman was told she needed additional clearance from the local authorities before she could go any farther. No, they did not know how long that would take.

In sweltering heat, with every single layer of clothing on our backs with which we had boarded the train in Paris, we left what had been a veritable pigsty home for nearly two weeks. On wobbly legs, we followed Maman to the café across the street from the station to make enquiries.

There, she bought us a small bottle of mineral water and, after a short conversation with the proprietors, left us in the care of the owner's wife. Meanwhile, she went looking for a place to live for the duration of our stay in Vierzon. Our fate was now in the hands of the Vichy authorities--and the French bureaucrats were rarely in a hurry.

Thus ended the first leg of our trip south in the hellish reality of survival under conditions of war. Each day of this surreal, miserable journey is permanently etched in the memory of the child I was.

#

Maman had to be very frugal since she had limited funds and did not know how soon she would have more. That's why she avoided the more costly hotels (which, in all likelihood, would have been filled with German officers anyway). Instead, on the edge of town and not far from the railroad station, she found us a little garret.

Upstairs of a storage building, it was accessed via a narrow exterior staircase. This tiny room had an electric burner and a small kitchen sink with running water but no other interior plumbing, and, as with so many of France's old semi-rural buildings, an outhouse was some distance away. Our garret had typically low, sloping ceilings with small screenless windows, and very simple furnishings. A kitchen-size, oilcloth-covered table was flanked by a couple of straight-backed wooden chairs. In one corner were two big cots; in the other was a tiny pantry. One bare light bulb hung from the ceiling in the center of the room. The smell of fresh paint lingered in the heat. But, though small, the most important thing following our cattle car experience was that our garret home was clean.

When she had reviewed the room and agreed on an acceptable deal with the owner, Maman picked up the key, dropped off our bags, and immediately came back to the station café to get us.

After introducing us to our new home, she instructed in a no nonsense manner, "Take off your outer clothes. I want you to lie down on the cots and rest while I go find out where I can buy food. Jacqueline, watch over the girls."

She was back a short while later and declared joyfully, "Get up; get up! Put on your shoes. We're going to go on a picnic. I am told there is a little pond near here. That's where we will go. It will be wonderful, you will be able to go swimming and wash off some of this grime." She waved her hand toward my legs and face.

Then, with her little brood at her side, she went in search of the bakery and delicatessen she had been told were nearby. She said she could buy what we needed there. She even found a little fruit--overly ripe and badly bruised but, with careful trimming, still deliciously refreshing. We had not seen fresh fruit for a long time. Here, in the central part of France where nearly everyone had their own gardens, it was easy to find such treats. The stringent Vichy controls already imposed in the North were only just beginning to be felt in Vierzon.

Maman packed everything neatly in a little basket that we found at a farmers' market. In her usual cheerful manner and with her artistic flair for presentation, she turned our picnic into a truly delightful occasion. A little fun was long overdue.

We went off joyfully for our first day of fresh air, sunshine, and recreation in two weeks. I was so happy, so lighthearted, ... and so filthy!

I still remember how giddy I felt at being able to walk freely with arms swinging wildly at my sides. My legs had nearly forgotten how to skip and run or take long strides. Though they were weakened from long days of inactivity, I could not keep my feet still; they seemed to have a life of their own. What freedom … what joy!

Along the way, to her sheer delight, Maman found a small, bluish-pink flower that she picked immediately. Then, she found another. She was now seriously hunting for it. I knew there must be something special about it to make her so happy. She showed me how to recognize it so I could pick some too. And, pretty soon, we had gathered more than we could handle.

"They lather up like soap." She chirped happily. "Since I have no soap left, we will use them to wash ourselves."

My Maman knew everything! I never questioned what she said because, in my experience, she was always right. So, although I was surprised to learn that a flower could be used as soap, I did not, for one minute, doubt her. In my mind, mothers knew all. And I was certain mine knew more than most.

We trudged along for a time through nearly dry fields. Now, we were walking along a dirt lane. We went around a bend, and there, in all its glory, was the pond!

What a dazzling sight. Secluded and totally at peace with the world, graceful willowy trees and shrubs surrounded its still waters. Rushes grew along its edge and down into the water itself. Floral perfume filled the air. Everywhere, there were sights and sounds of summer. Butterflies flitted here and there while dragonflies and damselflies hovered ever so briefly above the water before they suddenly left to flit elsewhere. Pond skaters, "Skitters," with their strong wings and long legs, glided and skipped along with abandon on the water's surface leaving behind gentle v-wave patterns. Bees droned from flower to flower and filled the air with a low buzzing hum. All blended together to provide a fitting orchestral background to the enthusiastic chirpings of birds hidden among the tufted rushes.

The sky was blue. The air was still. And the sun was hot. I couldn't wait to shed my clothes. I stripped quickly while Maman set up our little picnic site in the shade, not far from the water's edge. She put down a makeshift tablecloth and, in her inimitable fashion, promptly had a most appetizing picnic spread out. I remember the hard-boiled eggs among other things. I had always disliked them; they were dry and stuck in my throat when I tried to swallow them. Usually, I refused to eat them. But, this time, Maman insisted that I eat some. She said they were good for me. On this day, I did not mind at all; I almost enjoyed them.

Since we were too hot to eat very much right away, Maman agreed to wash the girls first. She filled up a small pail with pond water and set about the task of making her babies beautiful again. Just as she had said, the little blossoms we picked along the way did, indeed, lather up nicely. Maman washed Eveline first. She tackled Paulette's little behind next; it was such an angry red. As for me, she dismissed me with a wave of the hand and said I was big enough to take care of myself. When she was done, she cautioned us not to drink any water from the pond, and let us go in to swim and play.

The girls ran for the shallow edge. Since I already knew how to swim, I went for the deeper water where I washed myself with unbelievable relish. The cool water against my hot skin was pure joy. Only the bottom of the pond was disappointing; the soft, muddy bottom made footing slippery and uncomfortable. So, after splashing about for a few minutes, I decided to go finish my lunch. How refreshed I now felt.

"Chérie, go rinse the mud off your legs*."* Maman called out to me when I stepped out of the water.

I looked down. A few small blackish-brown muddy blobs remained around my ankles. I brushed my hands over my legs. One or two blobs came off, but ... Oh, *Mon Dieu!* The others moved! I screamed.

"Maman, Maman! *Viens vite.* Come quick." I yelled, panic rising in my throat. "Come quick. There are worms on my legs; they won't come off. Maman, come quick NOW!" I wailed, stamping my feet on the ground trying to shake off the little muddy blobs. Maman came running over to me and quickly assessed. "Oh, my God!" She exclaimed in disgust. *"Des sangsues.* Leeches!"

Without stopping to think, she yanked the remaining ones off. A few drops of blood began trickling down my ankles. She knew the bloodsuckers had only just attached themselves because they were still small. "That's why they're easy to remove," she explained. Stopping in mid-sentence, a look of horror suddenly came over Maman's face.

"Mon Dieu. Les petites! My God. The children !" And she quickly ran over to the little ones.

My sisters were happily playing in the water where they were sitting up to their waists. Maman ran in and scooped them out of the water. In a glance, her worst fears were confirmed. Eveline had been playing actively and had kept the water around her agitated. She only had a few of the little parasites on her and they were still small. But, Paulette, who had been sitting quietly in very shallow water, appeared to be covered from the waist down with what had by now become engorged little monsters three times the size of those that had attached themselves to me.

Maman put the children down and rushed for the picnic supplies. She quickly found what she sought. Salt! She sprinkled it liberally on the bulging slimy things clinging to Paulette, and to the ones on Eveline. Then, she did something I did not understand but that I had seen her do on previous occasions when something bad unexpectedly happened. Mumbling some words in Yiddish, she tossed a few grains of salt over her shoulder and spat several times in rapid-fire succession from the tip of her tongue.

When I asked why she did that, Maman explained that it was intended to ward off evil spirits, or a dreaded affliction. She said it was an old mystical Yiddish ritual she had learned from her mother who learned it from her own mother. She admitted she didn't know if it really helped, but she didn't want to take any chances

The salt did its work in very short order. One by one, the parasites fell off. Maman said the salt quickly dehydrates their tissues and makes them release their vise-like grip. She said you shouldn't pull them off once they have begun to engorge because infection can result.

Thus concluded the idyllic picnic that celebrated the end of our two-week cattle-car ordeal out of Paris. A memorable beginning to our sojourn in the town of Vierzon!

#

I don't recall being in Vierzon very long--perhaps a few weeks. I do remember going to see a doctor or a pharmacist who gave me medicine for the sores I had on various parts of my body. I remember being hot and crowded in our little garret. I also remember a very swollen, sore left hand where I was stung by one of the many wasps that nested under the eaves just outside our unscreened windows.

We kept to ourselves so that no one would find out we were Jews. Except for Maman's daily visits to the authorities to check on the status of our clearance request, we stayed close to home. Maman went to the post office every day. She had sent Papa a short message by post. Since the mail was heavily censored, they had pre-arranged some kind of code in the event of unexpected delays so that he would know our whereabouts. At some point, she received word back from him. Her trips to the authorities were now more hopeful. There was a spring in her step. Then, it happened at last; she got her clearance to leave Vierzon.

"*Hourra! Hourra! Hourra!*" I shouted when Maman announced her good news.

She was full of joy. I could sense her mounting excitement. We dropped everything to quickly repack our belongings. Her mood was contagious. I, too, became excited. We were finally going to leave the occupied zone en route to "Free France!"

This time there were no delays, though the train out of Vierzon was not a great deal better than the one we took out of Paris. Third Class would have seemed luxurious by comparison, but we did have wooden bench seats and we traveled a bit faster, though the numerous stops made me impatient.

There were always people who would leave the train when we stopped. Occasionally, some would board. These passengers were now mostly younger men. I remember one such man who didn't talk much to anyone. He boarded our car with a rifle and a knapsack. Though he put his pack down, his gun remained slung over his shoulder. He stood watch by the door all the time, a dark frown on his face as if watching for something or someone. Maman said he was probably going south to join a unit of *La Résistance* (the underground movement).

Now, because of the heat, the car doors were kept open all the time. It was invigorating to be moving, and our frequent stops brought an element of interest to an otherwise painfully lackluster existence. Some of the local women who waited at the station depots wore their traditional starched lace headdresses. They were so pretty. Each locality had a different and distinctive style of lace; I looked forward to seeing each new one.

"We will soon see our dear Papa, *mes Chéries*." Maman smiled her beautiful smile at us. "But we must get ourselves cleaned up first. Otherwise, he will never recognize us." She chatted on lightheartedly, talking more to herself than to us. She loved him so. Everyone who knew them remarked how much they loved each other.

We were not far from Toulouse, a major unoccupied industrial "Free-French" city some seven hundred kilometers south of Paris. It was in Toulouse that Papa was awaiting news from us, at an obscure little hotel, *l'Hôtel Bellfort*.

#

When we reached the town of Cahors (north of, and less than a hundred kilometers from, Toulouse), our trip was interrupted because Eveline had a brief intestinal illness. We stopped off there for one or two days to get the necessary medicines, and were on our way once more. Maman had mailed Papa a little note to let him know where and when to meet us. If we were not on one train scheduled to arrive from Vierzon, he was to come back the next day at the same time. It seemed hard to believe that soon, we would all be together again.

Maman wore a fresh summer dress; it fit her well and flattered her now-trim shape. Her wavy black hair, freshly shampooed, was nicely styled. In anticipation of seeing him, she had obviously primped more than usual. I wondered how she made her dark eyes glow the way they did this day. The lipstick she wore emphasized her perfect white teeth; they sparkled when she smiled. I noticed that she was doing a lot of smiling lately.

At long last, the day arrived! The train slowed as it approached the station at Montauban outside Toulouse where Papa had found housing for us. We craned our necks; the locomotive moved us closer and closer. Suddenly we spotted him. He was standing there on the small station platform in summer sandals, wearing a short-sleeve shirt and shorts with his jacket slung over his shoulder, and a big welcoming grin on his face.

What a tearful but joyful reunion it was. I was filled with indescribable relief. After all, if Papa was with us, nothing bad could happen; he always knew exactly what to do. As for Maman, her happiness was marred only by his account of the close calls he had while driving south with German fighter planes giving him chase. In early summer, the Germans had conducted seemingly endless strafing raids of the southern routes in order to stem the tide of French men leaving Paris to join resistance groups. Papa's car trunk was hit once. He said he traveled mostly at night with headlights off after that experience.

We stayed in Montauban for a few weeks. This was a critical time of transition for us. Pivotal family decisions had to be made, and we needed to put some fat back on our skinny bones. Here, food was readily available so we quickly regained our strength.

Other important health matters also needed to be addressed. The girls and I were treated for the rashes we had developed en route. I also developed a painful boil on my neck, the size of a golf ball. And, I recall having a persistent sore throat with a fever. These were all conditions for which I was treated in Montauban or in Toulouse. I still recall the exhausting, typically long wait in a public medical clinic where I had to have my boil lanced.

As for my sore throat, the doctor thought my swollen tonsils might be the root cause. At first, he talked about removing them. I cringed at the thought. Fortunately, he said it wasn't absolutely essential that it be done at this time, so we were given choices. Papa was anxious to move on but told Maman he would go along with what she thought best. Torn between Papa's strategic concerns and my short-term health needs, she turned to me.

"What do you think, Jacquiniou," using an endearing form of my name.

I remember swelling with pride at being consulted. Like a grown-up, I considered all my options. On the one hand, Maman felt I should get it over with. *Very sensible, but...* I mulled it over. She promised unlimited ice cream cones during my convalescence to soothe post-surgery soreness. *Hmm, very appealing.* When I asked the doctor, he agreed the ice cream bribe was a good deal.

On the other hand, he told me if I put off the surgery, I might be lucky and get along for many years without any more trouble. *A reasonable way out of an unpleasant and unwanted operation--for a quitter!* I considered all and chose to give up the ice cream. I placed my bets on my doctor's last point: do nothing! (I was such a coward.)

As it turned out, this was the right decision. Once the sore throat was gone, I had no further trouble. To this day, my tonsils and I are still the closest of friends.

In between such illnesses, the family made several short moves, including one to a rooming house in Toulouse. Through his business, Papa had contacts everywhere in France, and he was an active member of several organizations, many of which had their home bases in Toulouse. This industrial center in south central France had already become the destination of displaced Jews seeking refuge. And it became a natural choice for French and international aid organizations to set up headquarters there.

One of these was the *Comité d'Assistance Aux Réfugiés (C.A.R.)*. This was a refugee aid committee founded and largely funded by the Baron de Rothschild. At the time, C.A.R. was actively establishing subcommittees for refugee assistance in various cities and towns of southern France. Through its broad network, C.A.R. made sure the Jewish refugees in and around Toulouse learned about these towns quickly.

Otherwise, how could my father possibly have known about one of the best places in all of France to make a new home for his family: Luchon!

CHAPTER VIII

Luchon

Mes jeunes années	*My childhood years*
Courrent dans la montagne,	*Scamper in the mountains,*
Courrent dans les sentiers	*Scamper along wooded lanes,*
Pleins d'oiseaux et de fleurs.	*Filled with birds and flowers.*
Et les Pyrénées	*And the Pyrenees*
Chantent aux vents d'Espagne	*Serenade the winds of Spain,*
Chantent la mélodie	*Serenade the melody*
Qui berçât mon cœur.	*That cradled my heart.*
Chantent les souvenirs,	*Serenade the souvenirs,*
Chante ma tendre enfance,	*Serenade my tender childhood,*
Chantent tout les beaux jours,	*Serenade the beautiful days,*
A jamais finis.	*That never end.*
Et comme les bergers	*And like the shepherds,*
Des montagnes de France	*Of France's mountains,*
Chante le ciel légé	*Serenade the fair skies*
De mon beau pays!	*Of my beautiful homeland!*
Written by Charles Trenet	*Loosely translated by the author*

This once popular post-war song by Charles Trenet says it all for me. Each time I hear it, longing returns in my heart for a small mountain town deep in the Pyrenees called Luchon.

Ah, Luchon! At a time of great need, Luchon is where we found safe harbor and respite, however brief, from the obscenities of an insane war.

Surrounded on all sides by the majestic, but daunting *Pyrénées,* it is nestled snuggly in a sheltered moraine valley at an elevation of approximately two thousand feet. Its local governance is carried out through the *Département de la Haute Garonne,* one of France's many county-like subdivisions, administered by a prefect. At the time, barely three thousand souls made their homes there.

Luchon reminded me of tea leaves scattered along the bottom of a lovely china teacup. Its houses, farms, shepherd huts, and hamlets dotted the mountain-scape on either side of a young stream that bubbled joyfully through the village to meet its destiny below in the bed of the less impetuous Garonne River.

The townspeople were convinced they lived in the most beautiful valley of the most beautiful mountains of the most beautiful country in the world. Wool was a major industry and many of them were sheepherders with the characteristic independence and fierce patriotism typical of French mountain people. The other major industry was tourism; it included winter sports, thermal baths, and in summer, hiking and backpacking-- with a little diversion at the casino.

Luchon had everything. Most important to us, it was practically on the Spanish border with escape routes and trails close by. Papa said Luchon was the perfect place for our new home.

We arrived there in late autumn 1940.

I often wished that time had stood still during our first year there. As a nine-year-old tomboy, I could not have chosen a better place to live. That winter, I learned to ski and use a sled. I made the most creative snowmen in town, instigated exhilarating and always victorious snowball fights, and knocked down an untold number of obnoxious little boys on the ski slopes. I was a happy child again.

Maman occasionally took me to the thermal spa. She swore by mineral baths as the important first step in the traditional cures popular in Europe for treating rheumatism, arthritis, bad backs, gout, stress, and a host of other non-specific ailments.

We'd luxuriate for hours in the comforting warmth of the spa's natural sulphur springs. I loved swimming in the pool. It was always the right temperature--and what a great place for me to practice yodeling. I felt compelled to sing duets with my voice that echoed off the high marbled ceilings and walls. What a treat! I must admit, though, I wasn't wild about the odor. I didn't know about sulphur then, and wondered how anything so pleasant could stink so.

#

No matter what the circumstances or where we found ourselves, Maman always promptly set about reestablishing normalcy in our lives. Shortly after our arrival in Luchon, I was enrolled in school. I had missed one session during our flight from Paris, but Maman had kept me busy doing class assignments throughout our sojourn in the Toulouse area so I was not far behind my peers.

The texts and workbooks of the centralized French school system were standardized and each grade followed a pre-set course of study. No matter which school district we might find ourselves in, the lesson plan for a given grade was approximately the same.

The home schooling made it possible for me to continue at my grade level. I had little catching up to do. I even found time to doodle in class.

I had always loved to draw, even as a very young child. I took advantage of every opportunity to do so, especially during lackluster subjects such as history. Dates and places put me in a slumber zone. But the historic personalities themselves usually captured my attention. Doodles of the great medieval king of the Franks, Charlemagne, my personal *Gaulois* hero, with his lady at his side, were everywhere in my notebooks.

Despite my efforts to keep this extracurricular endeavor to myself, however, my sketches did not go unnoticed. I had not yet learned how observant teachers could be. One day, after seeing my doodles, the teacher asked me to come in after class. *Oh, oh.* I thought. *Now I'm in trouble.*

But rather than scold me for not paying attention, she asked to see the rest of my sketches. I blushed at having been caught in the act, but I was nevertheless flattered. Self-consciously, I showed her my notebooks; they were all filled with doodles. After looking at them, she urged me to enter a national upcoming competition that winter, which was sponsored by the Art Division of the National Department of Education.

At first, I demurred; I didn't think I was good enough. However, at the insistence of my teacher, I agreed (I really felt I had no choice if I wanted to stay in her good graces). So, I submitted a watercolor painting of a French warship proudly flying the tricolor flag in the Marseilles harbor. What else for a child in wartime?

Some weeks later, to my amazement (and my parents' bursting pride), I was awarded first honorable mention, the only student in my school to be honored. This was announced during a school assembly. A Vichy official presented me with a certificate of recognition signed by President, Marshal Philippe Pétain himself. I accepted my award modestly and, with a curtsy, said, "Thank you, sir." As I walked back down the aisle to my seat proudly clutching my prize, an impudent little voice in my head whispered, "An award from an anti-Semitic government to a little Jewish girl? Not bad!" I grinned and sat down.

Once my school needs were addressed, Maman had other plans for me. She wanted me to study music and was determined I take lessons, even though we no longer had a piano on which I could practice. Buying one was out of the question, so she created a makeshift keyboard on our table by putting chalk marks on it to denote black and white keys. When I objected to practicing on a table that couldn't sing, Maman insisted I try; she said this makeshift instrument would be nearly as good as the real thing.

For a while, as boring as it was, I did try practicing on my mute piano; I wanted to please her and learn how to make pretty melodies just like Maman. But, at my teacher's piano each week, it soon became obvious that I was not making the hoped-for progress. At home, my fingers could not 'hear' when they hit the wrong keys. My teacher's piano quickly figured that out. Pretty melodies were obviously not in my hands' future. The lessons and the boring practice, then, thankfully stopped. All I desperately wanted to do was to go outside and play.

#

That Christmas, our family was invited to our first-ever midnight Christmas banquet. And what a banquet it was! I had never seen so much food and so many goodies. How easy it was to forget these were not times of plenty.

What impressed me most was the table's huge centerpiece. There, in tantalizing splendor, sat the traditional *Bûche de Noël* (Christmas log) proudly displayed on a bed of evergreens. It was magnificent. This cake roll masterpiece was filled with whipped cream, covered with swirls of dark butter rum cream and shaved chocolate curls, and sculpted into a very real looking log. Yummm!

Maman could never have purchased enough food to put on such a lavish banquet. Our hosts, representatives from one of Papa's international organizations, obviously were not bound by the same government-imposed restrictions that controlled our own stomachs.

As a form of regulation, a *Carnet Alimentaire*, was issued for everyone in the household. This rations booklet entitled each of us in the family to a certain amount of foodstuffs. In our case, these did not meet the needs of our hungry, active brood.

However, the region being one of agriculture and sheep farms, we were still able to buy fresh produce and dairy products during that first year, as well as a little meat. Table wine, of course, was always available. There were vineyards everywhere in the South. Maman being the very creative and excellent cook that she was, managed somehow to find ways of making even the most humble of foods taste like prize-winning entries of Dijon's culinary competitions.

I remember one of her dishes as being particularly praiseworthy. Even in the best of times, organ meat had frequently been part of our meals; it was considered very healthful. Lamb kidneys, for example, she sautéed in very hot butter and served sprinkled with fresh minced garlic and chopped parsley-- delicious, and nutritious too. Another favorite was calf's liver sautéed quickly and served with a drizzle of wine and butter sauce.

But I had never been introduced to lungs before. Ugh! However, there were times when this tough organ was the only meat Maman could find. She tenderized it overnight in a wine marinade with herbs, followed by long slow cooking in lots and lots of red wine with onions and garlic. De-e-e-licious! We actually found ourselves looking forward to it. It was so reminiscent of her wonderful pre-war *coq-au-vin.* Instead, we now had *poumons au vin rouge,* veal lungs in red wine.

Not only did she have creative ways in the kitchen, her shopping skills turned up all sorts of wholesome, savory foods for us. Vichy was no match for her. She learned to purchase stale bread and make wonderful puddings with it. Cut up in small chunks and sautéed with onions and a lone cooked potato, it became a tasty and filling side dish for our family of five.

The milk that she purchased directly from farmers was not pasteurized so, to be safe, it had to be boiled. In the process of cooling, a rich creamy skin rose to the top; this, she skimmed and it became the butter on our breakfast bread.

She bought partly rotten fruit because often that was all there was left for Jews. From this would-be garbage, she retrieved small nuggets of pulp at their point of perfection. They were sweet, juicy pieces of fruit, ideal for a mixed fruit salad.

Thanks to her ingenuity, despite the near-poverty status and food rationing imposed on our family, we all managed to regain our general health. Still, following our two-week, summer train ordeal, it took a long time for the sores on our legs to heal.

By early spring of 1941, I was in good physical form again and wanted to explore everything. To the city girl I was, every turn in the village road beckoned. With a song in my heart, I'd go off to romp in fields bursting into yellow seas of wild lilies and jonquils. There, I lightheartedly threw myself down on the fresh spring growth to stare up at white clouds drifting lazily above. I'd remain on my back like this for hours while I blissfully inhaled the heady fragrance of the floral carpet around me, and dream of princes and princesses.

Sometimes, I went off to explore mountain trails, hopping across hidden brooks. Other days, I rode my bicycle along deserted country lanes and climbed every fruit tree I saw. I was in my element.

But, unfortunately, my season of pure joy was short-lived.

#

Early in the occupation, the Nazis had set certain things in motion for the control of the French population. One of these was the creation of a special institute in Paris totally funded by the Germans and set up to design, develop, and orchestrate propaganda against the Jews. This scheme would serve to fan old embers of French anti-Semitism in occupied France, give the people an outlet for their frustrations at being occupied, and provide scapegoats for their woes.

Films, posters, books, pamphlets, radio broadcasts, and newspapers appeared vilifying Jews in the most loathsome manner--even in the "Free Zone." Before long, we were blamed for all the economic problems that France now faced.

In the occupied zone, decree after decree was signed to further exclude and isolate Jews socially, politically, geographically, and economically. There, they lost all civil rights. Businesses were closed, and personal property was plundered or confiscated. Jews were not allowed to go out in public except to shop for bare necessities between three and four in the afternoon--a time when most stores were either closed or had depleted inventories. If Jews were found in violation of such ordinances, immediate arrest resulted. In other words, in the occupied regions, Jews could not become employed, could not operate their own businesses, and could not move about freely. They lost all means of self-support.

#

In the unoccupied zone, we knew of these developments as soon as they occurred anywhere in France. Fortunately, in Luchon, we could still function somewhat. Therefore, many Jews sought refuge here.

During our first year, Papa had been able to conduct a little business traveling around the region selling the remaining merchandise he had brought out of Paris. His travels, however, were not confined to business. Often, he was gone several days at a time. He had other important affairs on his mind as well.

I eavesdropped a lot in those days since it was the only way I had of learning what was going on. That's how I found out that Papa was active in several Jewish organizations and sometimes attended clandestine meetings out of the region.

Once, he was even sent to Switzerland as a delegate to an international Zionist meeting attended by notable personalities from Israel, England, and other nations. That was probably where he first met Dr. Schwartzbard, a Polish consular deputy from London. Papa was very impressed with this man, and their paths would cross again.

Even when he was home, Papa went to a lot of meetings. I was never told why, where, or with whom. I learned years later, that at least two American Jewish aid organizations had important bases of operations in Luchon: HIAS, the Hebrew Immigrant Aid Society, and "The Joint," the Jewish Joint

Distribution Committee. All of their activities, though obviously illegal under Vichy, were critical to our survival.

#

On August 20, 1941 in Paris, a first sweep of foreign-born Jews--or '*raffle*' as it came to be known--took place, organized by Vichy and the Germans. This was a devastating signal to all Jews in the occupied zone. It resulted in a new wave of refugees fleeing south. And, by fall, there were enough Jews in Luchon that a small congregation was able to organize High Holy Day services.

During this time we learned from a new congregationist who had just fled Paris that my Aunt Hélène, Maman's youngest sister, and her little son were picked up in Paris and deported to Auschwitz. They were never heard from again.

On Yom Kippur, we all fasted, as is the tradition for this solemn holiday, except for the little ones. In the morning, Maman went to early services. At the same time, she sent me out to take our place in the milk line. She planned to come relieve me later so I could go to services too. Maman and I often took turns standing in lines. By now, we had learned that, in order to have bread or dairy products in the house, we had to rise very early and stand in long lines for hours in front of the bakery or dairy. Otherwise, the day's rations would be gone by the time we reached the shops' doors.

I wore a beautiful new, pale blue outfit that day. It was a dress with matching coat and hat made of fine lightweight wool. Maman had it made for me out of a choice piece of fabric that Papa had brought from his Paris inventory. There had just barely been enough material for my size. I adored this outfit. It was perfect for the occasion and for this cool autumn day. It was the last truly fine outfit I was to have for many years.

I hung our empty aluminum milk can on the handlebar of my bicycle, and rode down the big avenue toward the shop in the central part of town. While I was pedaling down the street alongside the parked cars, I remember my stomach gurgling; I was terribly hungry. I had not eaten since the previous day.

Though I don't recall feeling light-headed, the next thing I knew, I was on my face on the pavement with my bicycle lying across my legs. I had passed out--perhaps from hunger--and fallen off.

Fortunately, this happened right across the street from the small local drug store where Maman bought medicines. The pharmacist saw me fall and came out immediately. He carried me into his shop to administer first aid to the many contusions on my face, hands, and legs. Then, after making me comfortable on a couch in the back, he gave me a light broth and had me rest. Since he knew our family, he sent word to Maman to come for me. Despite the mess I had made of my face, arms and legs, I had no broken bones or other serious injuries.

Unfortunately, I'd missed the milk line. Our family had no milk that day, and I never went to the service. Also, to my utter sorrow, my beautiful light blue outfit was ruined. I could never wear it again.

As time went on, hunger quickly became the driving force in all our lives. Once, during poor *Grandmère*'s final illness in Paris, and before she went to the hospital, she sent us a small bundle of two hard-boiled eggs. Having been wrapped lovingly in many layers of newsprint to insulate them, they were well preserved during shipping. She, who needed nourishment so badly herself, had sent us the black-market eggs she had managed to find. Her little note had simply said, "*Pour les enfants*. For the children."

That was the last time we were to hear from her.

CHASED BY DEMONS

PART FOUR

DESPERATION

CHAPTER IX

Dread and Pretense

By late 1941, the country's anti-Semitic mood had penetrated our own little village. The Nazis had increased their barrage of anti-Semitic propaganda through newspapers and national radio. Its pernicious effects were seen in changed attitudes all over town. Luchon was no longer the congenial, safe haven we had come to love. It had now become very unpleasant.

Signs of resentment and distrust were everywhere. Those who had been hospitable to us before began to look at us with contempt. We now had to be on our guard everywhere we went.

Papa cautioned, "We must become invisible. We must not call attention to ourselves in any way."

Maman grilled me every day, "Say nothing to anyone about your family. Don't trust anybody. There are people here who want to see us dead."

Derisive remarks were frequently made in school. I became paranoid. Is there anybody here I can trust anymore? Everyone became suspect in my eyes. I even became afraid to talk to my friends, so I distanced myself from them and no longer played outdoors. The quality of our lives reached a new low.

One day Papa decided the "time has come for the family to go underground." This meant that the people who had been known as the Grossman family had to "disappear." So, Maman and Papa changed their appearances. He grew a mustache and wore a beret like the locals; she adopted a new hairstyle and no longer used makeup. Then, with the help of one of Papa's organizations, we acquired false identification papers with pictures that reflected our family's new look. Our surname became Simon, an accepted French name.

Then, we left our old neighborhood and rented a two-story villa on the other side of town and quietly moved in. It was perfectly suited to our needs. Appropriately named, *La Villa Sans Soucis* (The Villa Without Worries), it was off the main road and accessed only by a dirt lane. With no traffic and few other homes nearby, our privacy was assured.

The house had been closed for a long time prior to our arrival. An entire village of homeless mice had found trouble-free housing within its walls. I was certain there were thousands of them. Though they were seldom seen, they were too often heard. Their merrymaking tormented and scared me all night long.

Except for these uninvited visitors that we hunted vigorously with traps, this was a lovely villa. A large, enclosed yard graced the front of the property and a tall cherry tree for me to climb shaded the house's entrance. The interior was spacious, airy and fully furnished. The living room had a fireplace, and the bedrooms upstairs had lovely views. All the rooms, except the kitchen, pantry, and bathrooms, had hardwood floors; the entire house was tastefully done. There was a big sink in the kitchen, and for cooking and baking, the biggest cast iron coal-burning stove I had ever seen. The stove even had a hot water reservoir. Since we kept the stove continually stoked, we never ran out of hot water.

In anticipation of new decrees by Vichy, we did everything we could to create an aura of being true *Luchonais* (Luchon natives) in this new house. Shortly after we moved in, with the help of some of our trusted gentile friends, we planted a garden. While the grown-ups plowed small furrows in the ground, my job was to cut old potatoes into large chunks, and make sure each piece had at least one eye ready to sprout. We placed these in the furrows, covered them with soil, and said a little prayer over them to ensure a good crop. We also cleaned up an old chicken coop that we found in the side yard, and acquired a rooster and chickens. We now had the necessary trappings to pass for long-time gentile residents: a vegetable garden, and an exhibitionist rooster to wake us at dawn.

As somber a time as it had become, there was a little brightness in my life. Caring for the chickens was a new experience and a source of fun. Each one had a unique personality. Soon, we looked upon them as our friends and gave them each their own names. The only two I remember were Blanchette and Cocotte. The rooster was simply *Le Coq*.

This menagerie occupied much of our day. At feeding time, Eveline and Paulette, with bags of chicken feed in hand, chased the uncooperative chickens all around the yard to get them to settle down long enough to eat out of their hands. The upstart rooster, not believing their purpose to be humanitarian--and not wanting to be outdone--chased Paulette and Eveline back to the house. Le Coq was very territorial. I usually had to step in to quiet everybody down. Even then, extremely possessive of his dominion, he always kept a sharp eye on us. All the while, he strutted about arrogantly amid his harem while his ladies, mindless of his verve and dash, pecked away at tasty tidbits on the ground.

Soon we had a few eggs in our diet and, after awhile, an ample supply of potatoes from the garden. Much later, to my chagrin, when we had to leave our villa, we even got boiled chicken!

But before that time came, Maman and I spent a lot of time knitting and sewing. She seemed eager to teach me how to do both. One day, I asked her, "Why must we fix all these stockings? Can't we just buy new ones?"

"We can't afford to buy new clothes now, even if the stores had some. That's why we must repair the old ones as long as we can." She replied matter-of-factly as she continued showing me how to darn the ever-increasing number of holes that appeared in my sisters' socks after each laundry day. I never became as good at it as she; her work always looked perfect whereas mine … well, at least my repaired holes were much smaller than when I first took my needle to them.

I didn't really like darning socks but I loved knitting with Maman. It gave us a lot of time together. I was fascinated with how fast she worked, pulling yarn out of our old outgrown knitted garments so we would have yarn with which to make new ones. First, Maman pulled the wool thread loose from the old piece to start it unraveling while I, with my hands about two feet apart, palms facing each other and thumbs up, caught and wound the free strand into a loop over my hands until, by winding it around and around, it became a thick skein. Next, Maman wound the yarn back from my skein into tidy balls. After weighing and labeling each, they were now ready for her next knitting project. She was a gifted knitter and a patient teacher. It didn't take long before, with great pride, I was able to wear my very first creation: a maroon scarf.

My sisters and I shared a bedroom upstairs. It included a sink, a luxury for us in a bedroom. Unfortunately, one night, the plug was left in the sink by one of the girls and the faucet's slow leak ran unnoticed. When I woke up in the early morning to go to the bathroom I found myself stepping onto a floating floor mat; water was everywhere.

My parents' bedroom was just below ours. When they got up that morning, they found loose wet plaster that had fallen from the ceiling onto their bed. Papa was furious. All three of us were severely punished even though I tried, in vain, to proclaim my innocence in the matter.

#

Many late night meetings were held in this house. Shutters were closed and drapes tightly drawn; only candles were used as a source of light. From outside, no light could be seen. Anybody on patrol would assume everyone inside was asleep.

People, usually men, came one at a time and quietly tapped a special signal at the door before they were allowed in. Maman always had a pot of chicory on hand; with coffee nowhere to be found anymore, this was the best alternative available. They all huddled around a powerful, forbidden short-wave radio that we had mysteriously acquired. Hushed whispers went on for hours behind the closed French doors of our living room. Perhaps they were trying to anticipate what might come next in this dreadful war and were planning accordingly.

I always found it difficult to sleep during those evenings. I was anxious and desperately wanted to know what was going on. Sometimes I'd summon my courage, take a deep breath and tiptoe downstairs into the central hall between the living room and the staircase to sneak a peek through the keyhole. If I couldn't make out much in the heavily draped, darkened room, I'd press my ear to the keyhole in my determined quest for information, but I only caught snatches and never fully understood what was said. Occasionally, following some of these meetings, Papa left and was gone for several days.

Whenever I asked Maman who these people were or what they talked about, she responded too quickly that it was not for little girls to know such things, and immediately changed the subject. Her behavior only heightened my curiosity. It also made me very wary of the world outside.

#

In December 1941 the Germans, through Vichy, staged another sweep of the occupied zone. Whereas before, they had only targeted foreign-born Jews, this time, they also picked up French nationals of Jewish descent.

Until now, Maman had thought that we, her French-born children, had government protection as citizens--although Papa was never truly convinced. Anticipating that the unoccupied zone would soon be subject to a similar fate, they became worried when they heard that the authorities would begin looking in the schools. In a desperate effort to keep me safe, and still be able to continue my education, they decided to put me where no one would expect to find a Jewish child: in a convent school.

The convent was tucked away on a quiet tree-lined avenue in a Catholic neighborhood conveniently located not far from our villa. But I was nervous about having to pretend all the time and I resisted.

"Why can't I just go to my regular school?"

"Times have changed, Jacqueline. The Germans have made everybody hate us so much that we now have to hide who we are."

"Why can't I hide at home?"

"Because, *Chérie*, if the Gestapo comes to search our house and finds a little Jewish girl hiding here, they'll arrest us all and send us to Germany. No, it's better to hide where they won't expect to find you."

"How do I hide who I am? I'm me."

Maman smiled ruefully. "Pretend you're Henriette, your old friend from Paris. Just don't say anything about Jews or where your parents were born."

"I don't want to go to school with nuns. I'm afraid. I won't know how to act." I whined. But I knew I had to do as she asked.

So, I was enrolled at the local convent school for the 1942 spring term.

Maman coached me about what I should and should not say. I was told to carefully watch and mimic the actions of other girls when the expected Catholic rituals were carried out.

Coaching also came from our gentile friends who went into much detail about what to expect. I practiced everything I was taught and nervously awaited the start of the term.

The day finally arrived. With my new gentile identity as Jacqueline Simon and great trepidation, I went off one morning to my first catechism class. A brand new crucifix was around my neck and the proper schoolbooks were in a backpack on my back. During my first days there, I pretended to be very shy and kept in the background. But I soon made friends, and after a few weeks I began to feel less nervous about the lies and the pretense. It seemed that I had been accepted as one of the Church's flock. Now that I felt more comfortable, I began to be my old assertive self again.

Unavoidably, there were times in class when I found it very difficult to keep quiet. Too many questions were raised in my mind during Religion instruction. I felt compelled to probe some of the Sister's premises since I knew first hand that, in reality, Jews were nice people. My questions about their role in the sad story of Jesus of Nazareth gave her pause.

"Weren't the Romans the ones who killed Jesus?" I queried, coming to the defense of my ancestors.

But the nun really raised her eyebrows when I asked, "How did the Virgin Mary get a baby if there was no regular Papa to help?" I had just begun learning about the birds and the bees; to me, "Immaculate" Conception didn't fit in somehow.

In the Sister's view, such inappropriate questions did not reflect the kind of home instruction expected from a devout Catholic family. She reported her concerns to the office.

Shortly afterwards, the Mother Superior asked Maman to come in for a conference. Apparently, it was felt that remedial instruction was urgently needed to put me back on the right path.

Maman knew trouble was brewing; we talked about it the evening before her appointment at the convent. From my daily reports, she knew what had prompted the meeting, but she was determined to try to salvage the situation. She was gutsy, my maman! It made me hopeful that everything would be all right.

The next morning, I watched from the window of my classroom and saw her arrive, walking tall and proud despite her short stature. She told me later that she did everything she could to be a convincing Catholic mother and to bluff her way out of an ill-fated situation. But she was unsuccessful and broke down during the meeting. In tears, she admitted the fraud and threw herself on the mercy of the Mother Superior. She begged the nun not to give our family away, to help hide me and let me remain in school.

Instead of the hoped-for understanding and sympathy, Maman received a hateful rejection. The nun refused to be of help. She declared that she would allow no Jews in her school, and under no circumstances was I to come back. This was to be my last day. Then, she summarily escorted my mother out of the office and the convent.

"Leave!" She commanded.

After standing watch to make sure my mother followed her order, Mother Superior marched across the courtyard to my building. She swept into the classroom. With loathing in her eyes and lips pinched, she came directly to me and yanked me to my feet.

In the most terrifying and humiliating moment of my life, this self-righteous nun, with contempt in her voice, and holding me up as if I were a dirty rag, announced to the entire class, "*Cette fille est une Juive,* This girl is a Jew--like the ones who killed our dear Jesus."

A gasp came from the students. And a stunned silence followed.

I was horrified. Trembling, I hung my head, fearful of what she might say or do next. I choked on my sobs and tears began to run down my face. The Mother Superior now called a recess for the rest of the class. Then, grabbing my ear, she pulled me out of the classroom. "Leave at once," she ordered as she dragged me out and across the courtyard.

My classmates all stood by, taking in every move. The Mother Superior dragged me out through the convent gate, and only there did she finally let go of my abused ear. By that time my friends had recovered from their initial shock. Abandoning their loyalty to me, they started jeering with the others. I was deeply hurt and felt betrayed; I thought they were true friends. Sobbing uncontrollably, I turned and slowly headed for home, forlorn and utterly humiliated.

Then, like a pack of snarling, hungry wolves, my classmates skulked out past the gate. I was mortified. A first stone was thrown; others quickly followed. In vengeful pursuit, with a barrage of rocks, they chased me down the street spitting and shouting, "Dirty Jew! Killer of Jesus! Dirty Jew!"

Mother Superior, a dour expression on her face, remained standing at the portal. Hands clasped together inside her sleeves, she watched stiff-backed in condoning silence while I, with my hands covering my head, ran away choking on my tears, dodging, screaming, "Ow! ... Please, ... Ow! Please, don't hurt me!"

The Nazis understood so well the power of hate. A common enemy around which to rally the masses and through which frustration can be vented is an effective tool for maintaining political control.

I still carry deep emotional scars from this experience. To this day, because the Mother Superior was its trusted instrument, I hold the Catholic Church responsible.

It was now mid-spring 1942.

#

The Nazis' plan for dealing with Jews had several significant phases. The first was the deportation of Jews to slave labor camps in Germany where many of them eventually became too weak to work and died from lack of food or medical care. Another aspect of their plan was to reduce Jews all over Europe to abject poverty so that what the Nazis claimed was a subhuman species would starve to death. Then, came an abhorrent climax to their ultimate plan, a successful test for mass gassing of prisoners in late 1941. This paved the way for adoption of their most draconian next step, *Die Endlösung der Judenfrage,* the Final Solution to the Jewish Question." On January 20, 1942, this infamous decree was adopted at a secret meeting at Wannsee, a Berlin suburb. It called for the unthinkable: the complete annihilation of European Jews--some eleven million--by systematic massive gassing. All at once, everywhere in occupied France, there were major sweeps of Jews.

In the unoccupied zone, Vichy applied new oppressive measures. In late spring 1942, all children over six years of age, were now required to wear a yellow Star of David with the word, *Juif* (Jew) sewn on it on the left side of our outer garments. The penalty for being in violation of that ordinance was immediate deportation.

Meanwhile, Vichy's hierarchy had a new national commissioner for "Jewish Affairs," Louis Darquier de Pellepoix, a known Nazi sympathizer. On his order, the first "Free Zone" sweep of Jews was carried out. From this point forward, ours became an unbearable existence too. Public places were off limits, and the dreaded one-hour grocery curfew was also imposed between three and four each afternoon. Foreseeably, as had been the case in the occupied zone, shops here were now usually found with empty shelves or closed during this hour.

#

One day, in keeping with the curfew ordinance, Maman and I left home at three to get groceries. But, after walking two kilometers to the center of town, we found the dreaded "sold out" sign hanging on the shop's door. Dejected, we turned around and headed for home since we had no other place to go for food.

Maman was beside herself. There was next to nothing left to eat at home. She grumbled and complained angrily about the *"salles Boches"* (dirty Nazi pigs) and what a dreadful existence we were forced to live.

Not far from the thermal bathhouse, we reached a main intersection. A German guard post had recently been erected there, and a young soldier stood on duty.

As we approached, he gave us a curt nod. Maman, still upset over the closed grocery store, glared at him and, muttering a few well-chosen epithets, spat on the ground in front of him as we walked past. I was dismayed at what Maman had just done. The yellow stars on our coats made me feel naked; I felt like a live target at a shooting gallery. Frightened, I grabbed her hand and tugged hard. "Maman. Let's go quickly," I begged, wanting to disappear from this possible threat as fast as possible.

But the damage had been done. A few minutes later, a local French gendarme stopped us. The incident had been reported to the French authorities by the German guard, and we were immediately taken to the local police station and placed under arrest. We had to explain our actions, provide identification, and show that we did, indeed, have money with which to purchase food. Jews who no longer had funds for sustenance, were immediately arrested for deportation.

Fortunately, the officers on duty were native to Luchon and not yet fully committed to Vichy's policies. They were not unsympathetic when they heard Maman's story. After summoning Papa to bring family papers verifying her story of the three children that needed to be fed, we were released. They gave us a temporary circulation permit so we could go home without being arrested once again, this time for being out on public streets after curfew. As we left, they warned us never to insult a German again.

Needless to say, Papa was furious with Maman. "Are you crazy? You could have both been deported and put to death." He yelled at her in front of me.

I had never thought of the German occupation in such an immediate and personally threatening way before. From that day on, raw fear was my constant companion; looking over my shoulder became instinctive.

It was now early July 1942.

#

That month, twenty-nine convoys of Jews from Paris were sent by Vichy to Auschwitz. This action was noted in the international press. As a result, a few comments critical of

French policies were heard from foreign officials. In response, Pierre Laval, the Vichy chief was quoted as saying,

"No man and nothing can sway me from my determination to rid France of foreign Jews and send them back where they originated. I will take no lessons in humanitarianism from any country."

Laval was fully aware of the Nazi's master plan when he made this statement. Unsurprisingly, sweeps of Jews to be deported increased.

Although the Nazi decree abolishing the "Free Zone" did not become official until later, in early November 1942 after the Allied Forces landed in North Africa, German soldiers were now seen everywhere.

With Luchon so close to the border, it came as no surprise that German headquarters were established here. Their growing presence was terrifying. As summer wore on, indiscriminate arrests of Jews became more and more frequent. Our family's fate was now very much in question.

The time for desperate measures had arrived.

CHAPTER X

Furtively, Three, on a Farm

Josie Cohen (I knew her as Madame Kirsch, a name she used during the occupation, possibly from a former marriage) was an energetic French lady of great courage and selflessness. It is thanks to Josie's humanity, and her outrage at what the Nazis were doing to Jews, that we survived. A gentile woman, probably in her early forties, she operated a beauty salon in town. Josie married a French-born Jew by the name of Simon Cohen, a highly educated practicing lawyer.

I believe this man may have been involved in high-level Jewish intelligence activities and was most likely in contact with the French underground. Undoubtedly, he also worked with C.A.R., Baron de Rothschild's committee for refugees. Through these connections, he and his wife, Josie, became good friends of ours. I recall that Papa thought him to be a brilliant man.

By late summer of 1942, this friendship was put to the test. German advance occupation units had begun house-to-house searches. According to their decree, any Jew found in hiding would immediately be deported or shot in the town square for everyone to see. Any gentiles caught hiding them would suffer a similar fate. Knowing that it was a matter of days before the full occupation of Luchon would cancel any remaining options, Josie, Simon Cohen and my parents made plans.

We shuttered our rented house. Using her beauty salon as a means of spreading the word, Josie let it be known in the village that our family had moved from Luchon permanently. Then, late one moonless night, under cover of darkness and after the town was asleep, we slipped out of our house. In ones and twos, so as not to put the entire family at risk all at once, we quietly and quickly covered the distance to her home. We glanced over our shoulders at nearly each step to make sure no one followed, and we moved into her basement.

There, she kept us hidden behind old crates of beauty supplies, trunks and other storage items while further decisions and arrangements were made. Meantime, in the streets above, the Nazis' house-to-house searches began in earnest.

In the days that followed, we waited quietly in our hiding place. We could only whisper so our sounds would not alert neighbors, and the girls were watched constantly to make sure they did not make loud noises.

One day, in early fall, Papa took me aside. Away from the girls, he soberly announced he had some very serious and grown-up things to tell me. My stomach tightened. I knew this could only mean bad news.

"You know, Jacqueline," he began quietly," these are desperate times; they sometimes require desperate actions of us."

"*Oui*, Papa. I know." I said solemnly, trying to sound as grown-up as I was able. I could tell this was difficult for him. I held my breath, fearful of what was to come next.

"Maman and I may have to leave Luchon without much warning." Groping for the right words, he continued, "We are all going to have to do things we don't want to do."

I sat up straight, my chest puffed out, "I will do whatever you want me to do, Papa."

He smiled sadly, "I know, *Chérie*. That's why I'm telling you what our plans may require of you." After a resigned sigh he continued.

"We may have to leave suddenly. If so, we will have to travel on foot by way of a hazardous and untried escape route. It would be too dangerous for you and the children, and there is no guarantee we would be successful." He paused and I saw tears well up in his eyes. I reached over, wrapped my arms around him and pressed my head against his chest so he couldn't see my own eyes filling with tears. He took out his handkerchief, wiped his eyes quickly and blew his nose as if to say, "Enough nonsense."

"What I'm trying to tell you is that Maman and I have decided it would be best if you and your sisters went away someplace for now, someplace where you will be safe." I panicked at these words and sat up. I opened my mouth to speak but I could see he had something else on his mind so I held my tongue.

"We will have to count on you to be brave and help watch over your sisters. Josie will be here. If anything happens to your mother and me, Josie has sworn to take care of you as if you were her own. Follow her instructions to the letter."

That was all I could take. Sensing the near hopelessness of our situation, I grabbed my father and cried out my grief into his chest as quietly as I could. No longer able to speak himself, he simply held me close for a long time and stroked my head gently until fatigue allowed me no more tears.

The next day, Papa and Maman told Eveline, Paulette and me, that they were sending the three of us to the country on a short vacation. We should immediately make ready to leave; we were to be on our way the following day. All they would say further was that they would make arrangements for us to join them as soon as they could. Taking me aside, they told me that, in the unthinkable event that they were caught trying to escape, we three would be in good hands. The wrenching truth of what I had just heard struck me like a bolt of lightening. A chill went through my entire body as, in near panic, I thought, *I may never see Maman and Papa again!* I wanted to object, but I didn't know what to say. What was the point? I understood our circumstances. There was no choice; all of our fates, my sisters', my parents' and mine, were now in the hands of others.

The following morning, after tearful goodbyes to Maman and Papa in the basement, my sisters and I made our way upstairs and, with our few belongings and Josie Kirsch's help, we piled into her car. I had such an empty, achy feeling in my chest as we pulled away from the house. *Is this the last time I'll ever see Maman and Papa?* But I fought back my tears; I couldn't let the girls see me cry.

We set out northward toward Toulouse on one of the back roads out of town in order to avoid running into German patrols-- which were more and more frequently seen now. As Josie drove, I looked anxiously back through the rear window at the road, praying with all my heart that we would not be followed by German patrol cars. My prayers must have been heard.

Some seventy miles later, we turned off onto a dirt road and pulled up in front of a small farmhouse. Josie told me this was to be our new hiding place. The farmers believed we were her children. She said she had told them they were hired to take care of us while she was forced to work long hours in her shop back in Luchon. They had no idea that the three little "gentile" girls now in their charge, all wearing silver crosses around their necks, were Jews hiding from Vichy and the Nazis. We said our goodbyes to Josie; she hugged us, and left.

Now began the greatest and most dangerous masquerade of our lives. Of the three of us, I alone understood. No parents, no family and no friends were here to guide us. We were on our own in a world that wanted us dead.

Thus came about our second wrenching family separation.

#

We lived on the farm from September to mid-December 1942. I went to school every day, to church on Sundays, and to Confession when I could not talk my way out of it. By this time, I knew how to play the game. Josie had coached me well. Despite the constant fear that gnawed at my belly, I was able to keep my farm hosts, my teachers, and the clergy in the dark. I had learned my lesson well at the convent in Luchon. I knew what to do, and not do, in order to avoid suspicion from church, school, and farm. I sought no friendships. I did not allow myself to get too close in my relationships with anyone. I held myself at a distance in school, discouraged my classmates from engaging me in idle chat, and kept my thoughts to myself. I became a loner who trusted no one.

My four- and five-year-old sisters were too young to grasp the circumstances, too young to understand what it meant to be a Jew in a world that sought the annihilation of their entire ethnic group. They were, therefore, too young to betray us unwittingly. They knew nothing. My parents and I had made sure of that. We had never discussed our plight, the War, or family plans in front of them.

#

As brief and impersonal as our stay was with our farm hosts, and as desperate as were the circumstances and the times, it was nevertheless a memorable adventure for me. I'd never had the opportunity to get close to farm animals before. After a short time, I developed a deep affection for them. There were several horses, a herd of cows, hogs, goats, geese, chickens, rabbits, cats and dogs. Each one had its own personality and many of them became special to me. I soon found myself thinking of some of them as my best friends. I knew these friends would not, could not betray me.

Our Sunday trips to church were among the most stressful events of my stay. That's when I felt most vulnerable; I was convinced everyone's eyes were on me. Memories of my ouster from Luchon's convent school were still fresh. I did not want to be pelted again, or be banished from the farm and placed under arrest.

Fortunately this experience was a totally different one. My farm family was discreet and thoughtful. Other than taking me to Mass with them on Sunday mornings, they let me make my own church-related decisions. One time, they asked me if I thought I was ready for Communion. Taken by surprise, I mumbled something unintelligible and demurred. But my hosts asked no questions. Their mention of Communion, however, created a moment of sheer panic for me since I knew nothing about it. Furthermore, I did not relish having a strange man, even if he was a priest, put a wafer in my mouth, no matter how hungry I might be.

There were no food shortages here, given the livestock available and the crops that we harvested. But, since this family was not compensated adequately by a stressed and struggling economy, the frugal household seldom hired outside help. Farmhands were mostly members of the family: the father, a brother, a couple of young sons, and a son-in-law. Few excesses were tolerated and everyone was expected to do his or her share. So, even though our hosts were being paid for taking care of us, I did everything I could to make myself helpful and blend in.

I took the cows to pasture and fed the farmyard animals. I milked the cows--with less than hoped-for results since my hands were not strong enough to pull and squeeze with the necessary conviction. I raided the chickens' favorite roosting places in the barn for freshly laid eggs that would feed the family. I cleaned out the rabbits' cages, taking my time while I chuckled at them and teased them with fresh lettuce leaves.

And I was taught how to force-feed the geese to fatten them up for Christmas markets. Ugh! Though a simple concept, this was a real challenge for me to carry out. The idea was to straddle a three-legged stool over the thankless animals and, while keeping their beaks open, force corn down their throats with the help of the rounded end of a sawed off broom handle. I did not relish doing this; they were strong, always tried to run away and I felt sorry for them. Clearly, they didn't appreciate the extra snack. As for the pigs, I had great pleasure watching them come running when I called them out of their house. They loved to talk; they'd grunt contentedly and occasionally look up at me as they slurped the slop I put in their trough. Afterwards, grateful for my services, they smiled.

Yes, I learned a lot on the farm. Everyone had his or her own *sabots* (wooden clogs). These were worn only outdoors and were kept lined up in a row on the stoop outside when we were in the house. The moment we went out, and before taking a first step onto bare ground, we had to slip them on over our heavy *pantoufles* (loafer-shaped slippers made of thick felt). With the mess made by the many farm animals outdoors--a mess occasionally transformed into a slimy mix of animal excrement and mud from frequent rains--we had to wear clogs. We'd merely slip them on or off our country slippers on our way out or in. That way, our interior floors remained reasonably clean.

We purchased my first pair of wooden shoes during one of the trips to the regional farmers' market early in my stay. Getting accustomed to them took some time. I had to learn to protect my insteps from the repeated pressure of the clogs' rigid edges. Otherwise, I'd get a bad bruise there. It took a while, but master that skill I finally did.

Every day, in addition to taking the cows out to pasture, I walked two kilometers each way to school in my clogs. I had to think ahead in case the weather changed, because when it rained, the walking was particularly challenging, especially if I took shortcuts across recently plowed fields. There, the earth was no longer firm and my clogs often got stuck in the mud.

Last but not least, with a great sense of accomplishment and without spilling a single drop, I learned to drink wine from a wineskin without letting its spout touch my lips. I had watched the farmhands carefully and studied their technique. Timing was everything. With head tilted backwards, I had to hold up the wineskin as far above my face as I could reach (with the spout aimed below my nose) and squeeze precisely at the moment I opened my mouth so it would catch the refreshing red stream hurtling down. Aim was critical; otherwise the wine landed wasted on the floor--or somewhere on my face. The evening I successfully and proudly demonstrated my new skill, I was heartily applauded. Just like one of the farmhands, I was slapped hard on the back in a congratulatory spirit of good fellowship; then, I was given my own little wineskin to carry at all times. I had become a true farm child, wineskin, wooden clogs, and all.

The farmhouse kitchen was a large multi-purpose room with thick walls of stone, and wooden plank floors that were frequently scrubbed with a bleach solution and yellow soap. A long, oilcloth-covered wooden table stood in the center of the room with an open bottle of local red wine always on it ready for the thirstiest among us. Flanked on each side by long benches, this table could seat twelve to sixteen people easily. This was where we gathered for our meals.

A huge hearth graced one end of the room and kettles of different sizes were hung above it. In November, when the weather turned cold, a welcome fire was ablaze all the time, and was large enough to have different temperature zones for varying stages of cookery. Two or more big kettles were almost always there, simmering--one with delicious-smelling country soups or stews, and others with the day's laundry. In the middle of the hearth was a spit. Often skewered on it was a choice piece of meat that was turned slowly to let the roast's oozing juices baste their source; every so often a drop fell and sizzled in the coals below, and a new mouth-watering aroma filled the room. Occasionally, the spit sported golden chickens roasting their way to perfection.

Sunday meals were happy, relaxed times. Everyone was dressed in his or her church outfit, the floor was freshly scrubbed, and the week's chores were behind us. When we returned from early Mass, if we liked, we could just go visit our animal friends. In a while, delicious smells drifted outside from the chimney, making my stomach gurgle and bringing me back toward the house. Time dragged until the clang-clang of the dinner bell finally rang at mid-day, triggering the expected stampede of farmhands toward the house. We could always count on freshly baked bread, a hearty soup, and a deep-dish fruit pie or bread pudding to round off the meal. Then, in keeping with French tradition, a large chunk of cheese accompanied by a jug of wine was the final touch to every meal.

In late November, the family decided to slaughter one of the hogs. I was beside myself. The target was one of my best buddies, but--as it was explained to me when I intervened in his behalf--he was not merely big and fat, he was also getting old. His time had come. Knowing what was in store, the family invited a couple of men from a neighboring farm to help. But *Gros Jules* (Fat Jules, the name I called him) was exceptionally smart. He understood French well and had excellent hearing. When he was called to step out of his pen that fateful day, he knew instantly that the jig was up. Screeching, he began running wildly all over the fenced barnyard with barking dogs and shouting men, all in hot pursuit.

The strength and skill of several men were needed to catch that poor hysterical, caterwauling creature once it had figured out there would be no tomorrow. After several minutes of frantic escapes from the final chase of its life, the coup de grace from a sharp butcher knife brought its terror and screeching to an end at last. Even more manpower was required to hang its massive lifeless form upside down. This was done so that the blood draining from its arteries could be collected.

The blood was later used for making *boudin* (black pudding), a traditional sausage popular among farmers. I simply could not bring myself to taste it. The preparation was, nevertheless, interesting to watch, even if it turned my stomach.

After the hog had been impaled on a spit and hung on a big iron hook in the walk-in cooler at the back of the house, a choice piece of its anatomy was removed and put in the hearth to roast. The womenfolk then took over the remaining food preparation and the tidying up while the men cleaned up the bloody mess in the yard. As for me, my job was to fill pail after pail with water at the outside pump for the cleaning crews that demanded endless quantities of clean water. I was grateful for this assignment; I didn't have to be too close to the stomach-turning mess inside. This slaughter was cause for celebration in the area. In the traditional manner for this region, it called for a festive meal with the neighbors. This meant good food with plenty of wine, lots of singing, a great many jokes, and much laughter. In other words, it was party time. As a member of the household, I was included in all of these activities, and was pleased to be readily accepted.

But I refused to partake of the *boudin* blood sausage when it was again offered, though I reluctantly accepted a helping of roast from the spit. Not only did I eat it, I thoroughly enjoyed it; it was delicious. I nonetheless felt doubly guilty--this had, after all, been an intimate part of Gros Jules, one of my best pals.

Furthermore, at the back of my head was the nagging thought, what would *Grandmère* have said? The little Jewish girl in me kept remembering what my grandmother had told me in Paris about the pâtés and ham that we adored. They violated Jewish dietary laws. Somehow, I had a sneaking hunch that those same dietary standards might also be in violation here. Not having any idea what the consequences might be, I was not prepared to tempt fate too much so I ate sparingly of the pork roast.

But, I had no qualms about other items on the menu, and I unhesitatingly accepted all wine refreshments. So much so, that by the end of the day, instead of waiting to be offered another glass of wine, I was refilling my own with abandon. After one such refill, I thirstily brought the glass to my lips and gulped down my wine unaware that my other hand was still tightly clutching the neck of the bottle. I was obviously anticipating my next *coup de vin,* a quickie it would seem. This slip of etiquette, from one so young, was immediately noted. It prompted explosive laughter along with teasing and much finger pointing at me, the young lush, sitting alongside the men at the table. The incident remained the farm's cause célèbre for some time afterwards.

On Saturdays, when the farmer or his wife went to the regional farmers' market, I was sometimes invited along. We saddled up one of the horses, stocked the wagon with vegetables and eggs, and went off for a half-day of trading. I enjoyed this activity very much. It provided a welcome change to the weekly routine.

But often, I felt blue and needed to be off by myself. When that happened, I had three favorite places to go. One was my bedroom, an oversized closet with no window, but it was my own private place where I could read, do homework, or simply hide. In it were a cot, a small makeshift nightstand with a chamber pot inside, and a lamp. My few possessions I kept in my suitcase under the cot.

The hayloft in the barn was another of my favorite places. I'd go up there and lie down in the straw, listening to the tippety tap of raindrops on the roof during the autumn downpours. The straw was soft, comfortable, and smelled wonderfully fresh. When I felt melancholy, I occasionally fell asleep there thinking of Maman and Papa. Except for the many flies that the cows below attracted, it was very private. When I was up there, no one could see me. That's also where I hid when an unpleasant chore awaited and I didn't want to be found easily.

But my most special place was the curving dirt lane past the farmhouse that led down to the open pasture. There, out of sight of the main house, was where my best friend, Roussette, spent much of her time. I knew I could usually find her under a tree near the fence, deep in thought. This gentle, russet-colored cow always came to greet me when I went out there to visit in the late afternoon.

She came close to me as soon as she saw me approach. She must have sensed how desperately I needed her wise counsel. There was so much I wanted to talk about. There were acts of anti-Semitism at school on the part of my fellow-students that I didn't want to bring to anyone's attention. This was a subject

Josie had told me to avoid. But I ached to tell Roussette about the nasty things I heard classmates say in school.

I also occasionally had complaints about some of the jobs I was given to do at the farm. "Why do I have to be the one to jam corn down the geese's throats? I don't like hurting them," I told Roussette. And, there were the trips to church every Sunday. I admitted I felt like I was betraying my family and my heritage. "Do you think I am sinning in the eyes of my Jewish God when I attend a Catholic mass? Do you think I'll be punished?" I asked my friend. She'd look at me with loving eyes and low softly; I took that to be a "No." I knew she understood.

I spent many hours with her, often tearfully, sometimes spewing angry torrents against an unjust world, other times pretending Papa and Maman were coming to get me. She was such a great listener; I always felt better after our long talks. Roussette was never judgmental and she always agreed with me. These visits were vital to me because she was the only one I could really trust.

Of all my animal friends on the farm, I loved her best. Not only was she loyal and trustworthy, she was comforting, ... and so discreet.

CHAPTER XI

The Dark Journey Begins

The Christmas holiday break from school had just begun when the call came from Josie Kirsch. We were to pack our things and go home for Christmas, but we would be back after vacation, she said. I took her at her word and didn't pack everything; I left some light summer-weight items behind. In any event, we did not have much with us at the farm. Most of our belongings had been left at Josie's.

I sensed something important was in the air. When she came for us, we bid our goodbyes to our hosts and said we would be back in a few weeks.

Josie and I whispered all the way back to Luchon in the car she had hired. I was full of questions. "Where are Maman and Papa?" was the first query out of my mouth. She told me that they had left her home in early November under cover of darkness. When I asked what they had done with our family's things, she put her finger to her lips and whispered that they had buried their most precious documents, family pictures, and jewelry in her backyard. They carried everything else on their backs and left on foot.

With the help of a local shepherd guide, they took the shortest route to safety in Bossost. This Spanish border village, though barely ten kilometers from their Luchon hiding place, was reached via a steep, arduous climb at night over obscure paths.

We finished the couple of hours drive to Josie's home. Just before we arrived, she leaned toward my ear and whispered, "You will soon see your Maman and Papa. But do not to say a word to your sisters. Now, I cannot tell you anything else. So, no more questions." I was so excited that I could hardly sit still.

Maman and Papa are alive. I am going to see them again! I shouted silently to myself.

By the time we arrived, it was dark and too cold for anyone to be out. A light snow had fallen. Looking furtively down the street to make sure no one was there, she quickly ushered us down to her basement, our brief home of three months earlier. There, she fed us and put us to bed. She said we should get lots of rest as we were going to need our strength. Of course, we did as she asked. But it was hard for me to fall asleep; there were too many questions running through my head, and I couldn't stop thinking about seeing Maman and Papa soon.

Josie must have repacked our things while we slept. When she awakened us, our three suitcases were shut and strapped. Our warmest clothes and heaviest shoes were laid out for us.

I quickly put on my belted wool-jersey maroon dress and tucked it into my ski pants. Over my dress, I slipped on the wool sweater that Maman had knitted. Next, I put on a scarf, four pairs of socks--most of which I had darned myself--and my ski boots. My heavy navy winter coat, knitted hood, woolen gloves and waterproof mittens were among the last items I put on.

Eveline had similar clothing, some of which Maman had also knitted before her departure. As for Paulette, her outfit consisted of several layers of jersey flannel underclothing, thick knitted leggings with matching sweater, a hooded cap and mittens. Since she had no other winter shoes, heavy wooden clogs were slipped on over several pairs of thick socks.

We were given some bread and hot milk; then, we were quietly taken to an old car waiting outside. Someone I didn't know was at the wheel. The motor was running but the lights were off, and for much of the drive, they remained that way. Darkness was total; it must have been around midnight. Our three small bags had already been loaded in the back.

Josie accompanied us. She made us as comfortable as she could; and after covering us with an old blanket, we were on our way. The girls were soon asleep again.

No one had seen us arrive. No one saw us leave. Josie told me that we would be making a long and difficult journey. Therefore, it was important for me to have as much sleep as I could get. I knew intuitively that the coming nights would be trying ones, otherwise, why all the heavy clothing and the sneaking out in the middle of the night? I was filled with anxiety. But, despite the dread of what lay ahead, there was an undeniable element of anticipation and excitement. I was going to see Maman and Papa again!

I don't know exactly how long we drove that night, but I do know we were headed east in the direction of the Mediterranean, on a road I had traveled with my parents. The motion of the car was soothing and despite my anxiety, after a time I, too, fell asleep.

It was three nights before Christmas.

As the night wore on, I lost track of time and place. In part, this was due to my frequent naps. It was also because of the circuitous route our driver took. Josie said he chose this route to made it more difficult for us to be followed. Such precautions gave me a deepening awareness of the grave danger we all faced.

Josie had told me about the current state of the occupation. I knew the Nazis and Vichy were now hunting every Jew in France--in the south as well as the north--whether foreign-born or not. Furthermore, "*les Boches*" were now also hunting those non-Jews who hid them or helped them escape. The lives of these good people were as much in jeopardy as ours. Josie told me the Gestapo had decreed that anyone found helping Jews would immediately be executed in the town square. Now, I feared for Josie too.

Eventually, we reached what must have been the little town of Tarascon-sur-Ariège. The rail line that services the lower Pyrenees, between Foix to the north and Ax to the south, passes through this town. Our interim destination was the railway station. With headlights off, our car stopped nearby on a dark little road where it would not be noticed, and we got out. Then, with our bags, we headed off on foot.

Though it was well into the night when we reached the station, the train platform was teeming with humanity. There was trash everywhere. Many people were lying down on the ground, leaning against walls or posts, or sitting on makeshift parcels trying to catch a few moments of sleep. Apparently, they had been waiting a long time for the train that, as it turned out, was not expected for several hours. Josie said train schedules no longer meant anything since the German occupation of the southern zone began in November. It was not unusual to wait several days for a train, and no one wanted to miss this one. The scene was stark and too familiar. It reminded me of another, more chaotic but equally fateful departure two years earlier from Paris, except this time we were outside in the bitter cold of winter, and Maman was not with us.

We found some free space at the far end of the platform and made ourselves as comfortable as the cold night permitted. I looked around and realized how lucky we were. Many had light clothing on; ours was warm and protected us from the cold biting wind. Others lay exhausted on the ground trying to sleep, newspapers spread over them for warmth, while we were well rested, having slept all day. Nevertheless, I did doze off after a while, my cold nose covered by my woolen scarf, and my gloved hands tucked inside my coat sleeves.

Our southbound train arrived in the morning. It was a crowded, third class train. Still, everyone was able to board it, and we were finally on our way again. The trip was short. When we got off, we were met by one of the guides Josie had told me about. I had never seen this man before. Josie told me to follow his instructions exactly from this point on. Her dark eyes gave me a long, lingering look; then, she hugged and kissed us goodbye. After some brief instructions to the man in whose hands our fate now lay, she was quickly gone. I knew from the mixture of compassion and anxiety I saw on her face when she left that she was asking herself, as I was, if we would ever see each other again.

From this point forward, Eveline, Paulette and I were in the hands of strangers. We were taken in an old car up a long winding road. It seemed an endless ride, but eventually we reached a stone hut, our first mountain relay point. The road apparently ended here. It was now late afternoon and darkness was nearly upon us. We were fed, and put down on cots to sleep. When we were awakened, it was pitch black outside and time to be on our way again.

The next leg of our trip, farther up the mountains, was by mule cart. The three of us were told to lie down in the back alongside our bags and in the middle of boxes of provisions stacked on each side of the cart. To hide us from view, several layers of sheepskins were put over us.

"Make no sounds." We were told firmly.

"*Oui, monsieur.*" I said quietly from beneath the sheepskins. But to myself I began to worry about what I could do to keep my sisters quiet if they became restless. However, the pitch and sway of the cart rolling along over the mountain trails was soothing. Soon, they were asleep again and never made a sound.

Hours went by. Sometimes, the cart stopped and, through the layers under which I lay out of sight, sounds of brief, muffled conversations reached my ears. At such times, fear gripped my insides. I was sure that any moment someone in a uniform would yank back the skins that hid us. Occasionally, the guide would come back to check his "cargo," or make a short inquiry. Then, we would be on our way again. We drank no water, ate no food, nor were we offered the opportunity to relieve ourselves.

The cart now jostled and lurched frequently as it made its way over the rocky trail. The mule, steadfast and surefooted, plodded unerringly ever upward. In our hiding place, I imagined we were being kidnapped and, despite my resolve to be brave, tears sometimes filled my eyes. Then, I told myself I was being silly and I tried to imagine being in Maman and Papa's arms again. Just as I was beginning to despair that this trip would never end, the cart stopped. Finally, we had reached our destination, our second relay point. What relief to be able to move at last, and to go to the bathroom!

We were now at an even more modest and remote shepherd's hut. We entered as we were told but no names or information were exchanged; we were simply fed and put to bed. Since I did not understand the ancient mountain *patois* language of these people, eavesdropping was pointless, although my curiosity urged me to do it. I had to settle for the few words spoken to me in French when there were instructions given. Any questions I asked were answered with the fewest possible words, and in a manner leaving no doubt that further discussion would be unwelcome and unlikely to follow.

These private people guarded themselves well; they did not trust strangers. Their own survival depended on discretion. "The less said, the better" was the conventional wisdom. So, we were kept in ignorance.

Somehow, I was able to sleep more during that day, as did my sisters. Was it possible that we were given something to help us sleep so we would be well rested for what lay ahead? When we woke that evening, there were more men in the hut. All wore the characteristic well-used blue berets typically seen on the country folk of France. Also, there were now some other, older children. They spoke a foreign language, but they were dressed, as we were, for travel in the cold. I had the impression that they, like us, were also escaping and would be part of our group.

We were fed again and given hot milk to drink. At the end of our meal, we were told to prepare to leave and to put on our warmest clothes. I did as I was asked. But when I put on my ski pants, I noticed they were now a bit loose around my waist.

They must have stretched since I first put them on, I told myself. Since I had no other belt, I looped the cloth belt of my maroon dress onto my ski pants and tied it in a secure knot.

I was given some old newspapers and instructed to put layers of this newsprint inside my ski boots under my feet for insulation, and I was also told to be sure to put my gloves on before putting on ski mitts. I followed all instructions as I had promised Josie I would do. Finally, I put on my wool hood, the wool scarf around my head and face, and my winter coat over all. With all this, I'll probably be too warm, I thought.

Paulette, now dressed like a stuffed doll in several woolen layers, had been crying constantly. In normal times, it didn't take much to make her cranky. Now, she was probably in a bad mood because she hadn't had any exercise and didn't like all the strangers milling around her. She was soon given some warm red wine to drink. It seemed to soothe her and after a short while she settled down once more.

The guides were now getting ready to leave. Each wore a thick sheepskin parka and carried one or more backpacks, along with picks, ropes, and a long walking stick. I was given a small pack to carry on my back as well and a ski pole for support while hiking.

Just before we left, I was pulled aside by the lead guide, Monsieur Jean, a tall man in his middle years, with chiseled features bronzed by years of exposure to the elements. Though he was a bit gruff, I sensed him to be a caring man.

"This is going to be a dangerous crossing. We will be climbing on foot all night. The cold and wind are very harsh and you may get so tired that you'll want to lie down and rest. But you must never do that." He warned. "When people lie down in the snow, they fall asleep and seldom wake up; they can die."

Fear gripped my heart.

He continued, "Once we start, we must keep walking. We won't stop often. Follow the guide in front of you and step only in his tracks. Do not make new ones."

"Why?" I could see he was impatient with this little delay of mine.

"Narrow tracks are not as easy for a border guard to see from a distance. Also, the mountain people who live in these parts often make such tracks while they go about their work. The guards know this and ignore their tracks. Now, enough questions."

He warned further that we must all be very quiet. "There is to be no talking. Sound carries in the mountains. Try not to cough or sneeze, but if you must, be sure to muffle it in your coat. There are Nazi Gestapo checkpoints along the way. Sometimes they have bloodhounds with them. The slightest noise could give us away. Then, you might never see your maman and papa again."

His words terrified me. The image of a snarling, salivating black dog flashed in front of my eyes. What chance would I have against a mad dog? I summoned up my courage and pushed the image out of my mind.

As for the cold, I felt quite capable of enduring it. Had I not lived in Luchon for two winters and knew how cold it could be in the mountains? Had I not played in the snow for hours and learned how painful my thawing fingers and toes could be afterwards? I was prepared for that.

Standing with clenched fists and gritted teeth in the safety of the hut, I resolved to outwit the Gestapo guard as well as his dogs. I also promised myself I would stay alert and not fall asleep along the way. Then, I stepped out into the dark cold night. I was ready.

CHAPTER XII

Darkest of Nights

Christmas Eve 1942

I learned later that this date was chosen deliberately. Border guard posts were not likely to be heavily staffed on Christmas Eve because, under the best of circumstances, that assignment was a lonely one. Those German soldiers who drew this holiday duty would probably be in a nostalgic mood, their heads filled with thoughts of former Christmases at home. No doubt they would be drenching their homesickness in numerous steins of contraband beer. Thus anesthetized, they would not be very alert.

Before we set out, the head guide assigned each of us the specific order in which we were to walk along the trail. A big guide with baggage strapped to his back was in the lead. He was the one who would cut the narrow trail and establish the pace for the rest of us to follow. Next, in single file, went the small group of foreign children who had mysteriously shown up after our arrival, followed by another guide with packs on his back. Then, came a guide with our packs. Behind him was Paulette, carried on the back of her guide. They were the ones I was to keep my eyes on. And last--to make sure no one went off trail--was our head guide carrying Eveline.

Our trek began. The sky was laden and the air was cold. Snow had fallen; a fresh layer covered the trail. The velvety stillness that enveloped these mountains was at once comforting and threatening. Evergreen trees whose branches drooped with new deposits of snow hugged the trail. Their shadowy forms assailed my imagination. Beyond them, I could only guess what eerie mountains rose around us. Friendly though they had seemed in Luchon, now I found them to be hovering menacingly all around me.

We walked in silence, stepping into each other's footprints as we had been instructed. I could not tell from these tracks how many had walked the trail before me--neither could anyone who might be tracking us. The freshly fallen snow was not deep; walking wasn't difficult at these relatively lower elevations. The pace was steady and slow and I kept up easily at first.

Soon, however, the gentle slope became steeper and my breathing more labored. No one spoke. Occasionally, I glanced behind me to make sure Eveline was still there. Ahead, Paulette seemed to be sound asleep on the back of her guide. They had gained ground and were further ahead now. I worried about my sisters and wondered if they might possibly freeze. I remembered Maman saying, "You must move your arms and legs a lot when you're in the cold to keep your blood flowing."

We walked in this manner silently for two or three hours, climbing gradually. Suddenly, we stopped. My hands and feet were now quite cold despite the double gloves and the layers of newsprint lining the insoles of my boots. I had begun to feel the fatigue that I was earlier told to expect, so I was grateful for this short rest. But I quickly learned that our stop was tactical, not humanitarian.

The guides conferred in hushed tones. Apparently, the first Gestapo guard post was not too much farther and it was now critical to be extremely quiet. After scouting ahead, one of the lead guides came back with more bad news. A trained police dog was there as well. Our lives now depended on each one of us doing our part perfectly. The dog must not hear a sound or pick up our scent. Otherwise, it would all be over.

We walked on. The wind started to come up. What had been cottony silence now became a low eerie whistle. We were nearing the broad, saddle-shaped pass that we had been told about, but this col and the guardhouse that secured it were as yet hidden from view. Snail-like, we continued our approach. The trees and boulders that had given us cover began to disappear as we gained more elevation. I strained my eyes to see what lay ahead. Despite the dimness of this starless night, the snow reflected ambient light. Ahead in the distance, a vast snow-covered expanse slowly came into focus. Nearly in the center of that desolate place, a tiny box-shaped hut could be seen: the dreaded guard post!

The plan was to cross the col upslope several hundred meters to the right of the guardhouse. This would put us downwind of it since the wind was blowing up from the left. Any sound made by our group would be carried away from the hut. Crossing the exposed slope was to be done one at a time with about two hundred feet between each of us. With that much space between us, the one following would still have time to retreat without being seen should the need arise. Once across, we were to seek shelter out of sight among the boulders of the large stone outcrops on the other side. There, we could rest until the others caught up.

A small adjustment was made in the group's bearings; we circled slightly until we felt the wind blowing in our faces from the direction of the hut. Crouching low in the snow as we approached the perimeter of the exposed col, we stopped, hunkered down and waited. The lead guide signaled each of us, one by one, when it was our time to cross.

I watched, breathless, my heart pounding in my ears. My eyes went back and forth, first to the hut then to the hapless hikers on the exposed slope. Why, I thought, did they move so slowly? Why didn't they walk faster? Didn't they know how vulnerable they were? I watched first one then another little figure move, cat-like, the several hundred feet to the far side. At any moment I expected to hear the sentry's feared, "Halt!" blasting through the mountains, immediately followed by the deadly snarls of a vicious killer-dog.

Suddenly, it was my turn to go. My heart was in my mouth. In a moment of panic, I wanted to run away. Terror captured my soul, cowardice gripped my legs and, for an instant, I couldn't move. My heart raced and despite the cold, I was sweating. Thoughts ran pell-mell through my mind. Can I make my feet move? Will I be the one to make the killer dog bark? If he does, what will I do? Where should I go?

Then, in a slow-motion manner, I took my first step. Robot-like, I took a second one, then a third, following the narrow foot trail cut by the others into this otherwise pristine blanket of snow. By the time I was halfway across, the snow was above my knees. Wind gusted sharply. Each time it blew, I nearly lost my balance; I felt like I was trying to walk a tightrope.

The hut was now in full view down slope to my left and faint sounds from a radio carried on the wind. Inside, there was a light and I smelled smoke that came from its chimney. In this barren white universe, I felt so alone. I could hardly breathe. In fact, I dared not breathe too deeply; I was afraid the dog might hear me.

With senses strained to detect the slightest sign of trouble, I inched my way across the slope. I kept asking myself why the distance was so much greater than it had appeared. I looked up to see the small, distant figure of the guide on the other side encouraging me on and signaling me to hurry. Oh, how I wanted to be able to run the rest of the way!

Fatigue was beginning to overcome me. My left ear felt frozen. The wind had now reached near gale force over this part of the slope and was thrashing its way inside my coat. To add to my misery, a wet snow had started falling and icy needles buffeted my eyes and cheeks.

Finally, after what had felt like the longest walk of my life, bleary-eyed I reached the shelter of the rocks. I couldn't even feel victorious; I was spent.

#

After I had made my way safely across, I crumpled gratefully into the snow to rest. My sibling inventory reassured me that all was as it should be, though Paulette was well ahead of me by now. Within a few minutes, the lead guide, with Eveline on his back also finished making the crossing. No sooner had he reached me than he made me start walking again, and prodded me to catch up to Paulette's guide.

I did as I was told and pressed forward once more as fast as my legs and lungs permitted. The snow nearly covered the tracks now, making things more difficult. I was afraid that I might not be able to see my way and would lose my little sister. But after a very long while, I caught sight of them again.

Her guide had slowed down for one of our rare rest stops. Paulette was still fast asleep on her host's back; she was totally unaware that she had lost her right clog. I approached her and quickly removed my glove to check her foot. It felt very warm so I assumed she had just lost the clog in the past few minutes. I asked the lead guide if I could go back to look for it, but he was absolutely unwilling to let me, or anyone else go. My pleas were to no avail. Paulette's little foot now only had the protection of several pairs of socks. In this cold, I worried it would freeze.

#

The Gestapo's first guard post was, by this time, far behind us. Tree line was long gone; instead, huge boulders were everywhere. We continued to climb. We must have been above seven thousand feet when, not far ahead and to our right, the dark outlines of sharp craggy peaks suddenly loomed higher still. Thinking I might have to climb those as well, I became utterly depressed. I could not possibly do it.

"Do we have to climb up there too, Monsieur Jean?" I asked the guide plaintively during a brief lull in the wind.

"*Non*." He said. "That is Andorra. But we must not attract attention as we pass by. There are *beaucoup de brigands*, many nasty thieves, who live up there. We don't want them to know we're here, so, let's be very quiet."

This response did not make me feel a whole lot better, but at least I wouldn't have to climb those crags. We pushed on.

The guides were staying close together now. Earlier, before the wind had become brutal, I had covered my head and face with my scarf and tied it securely behind my head. Despite this protective cover over my nose, I was starting to have trouble breathing. The back of my nose hurt, my throat felt as dry as tissue paper, my lungs rebelled against the icy air that penetrated the wool each time I took a breath, and my chest felt as though it would burst.

I kept my head down against the freezing wind. Pounding us ceaselessly, it also kept drifts in constant motion. Most of the time, in order to see, I had to squint through my eyelashes since I had no goggles to protect my eyes from the whipping snow. Here, there were no more trails, no more tracks, only the gusting snow and howling wind.

Oh, how I ached. *Am I going to die here? Is this biting cold and wind-swept slope going to be my grave? Is there nothing left for me but this violent, barren place?* I asked myself.

My fingers and toes were completely numb. Throbbing pain in my legs made them balk at each step. My face felt like it had been scraped with a hot knife. As for my lungs, they couldn't process any more air; they felt nearly frozen.

By this time, it was perhaps three or four in the morning. The only thoughts in my mind now were weariness, weariness and weariness. My legs felt leaden. I kept repeating to myself, just one more step ... just one ... more ... step... just ... one... I paused briefly to look up. *My head is so heavy, but I have to see where I'm going ...*

Ahead, through bleary eyes, I saw the outline of another steep climb. I became utterly dejected. More snow ... rocks ... wind ... I dragged my unwilling foot forward. I couldn't think

… that was it! I simply could not fight anymore. My legs and will were spent, my body surrendered. I gave in to despair and collapsed. The moment I came in contact with the ground, the illusion of warmth and comfort that my addled mind and the snow beneath me created was overpowering. Delicious sleep overcame me immediately.

Suddenly, strong hands were shaking me vigorously, jolting me out of merciful sleep. I sensed what was happening but my brain resisted; I could not wake up. Several slaps across my face finally brought back full consciousness.

Fortunately, Monsieur Jean had not been far behind me. He dragged me to the protected side of a large boulder and continued ministering to my needs. "My legs hurt too much to walk and I can't feel my feet," I complained. So he rubbed them vigorously until I soon felt sensation flow back into my abused limbs. He then gave me sweet candy and a drink of wine from his pack, all the while scolding me for not heeding his words of caution. I could tell he cared, and I felt drawn to him because of it. Strength somehow slowly returned to my limbs and I was able to start walking again; but from then on, Monsieur Jean stayed right behind me.

#

Before dawn we passed two other guard posts unseen. These were not as potentially dangerous as the first because they were only French frontier guards. From this point forward, our passage went without incident … except for one unforgettable event that was immensely humiliating for me.

We had walked all night with very few breaks. "Relief" stops had not been permitted once we had reached the highest elevations. Now, as we approached the Spanish border checkpoint, our final hurdle, I felt a pressing need. But, our guide thought it imprudent for us to stop at this time.

"We are close to a successful crossing; but we are even closer to dawn." He said. "This is the time people begin to stir in these mountains. I don't want to risk a delay of any sort until we reach safety. Can you hold on?" He asked with care in his voice. I nodded woefully with clenched teeth.

"We're almost there. We only have another few minutes of walking." He promised.

Not wanting to be responsible for the failure of our crossing, I squeezed my bladder muscles as hard as I could and kept walking. The "few minutes," however, felt closer to an hour to my nearly exploding bladder; but Monsieur Jean made good on his promise. When we reached the other side of the summit area where he wanted to be before dawn, he gave me the go ahead sign. By now, I was truly desperate.

I pulled off my gloves and quickly went off the trail and out of view. While I was looking for a private spot, I was also frantically trying to untie the knot of my jersey-knit belt that held up my ski pants. My numb fingers were clumsy and I couldn't see clearly as it was still fairly dark. Tears of frustration began to fill my eyes, making matters worse. Suddenly, to my utter dismay, my overburdened bladder could hold no longer. The tears I had held in partial check suddenly ran freely down my cheeks in tandem with the other most unfortunate flow now running down my legs.

Thus, standing tall atop the Pyrénées with the Nazis outwitted and successfully left behind, I met a new country, a new day, and a new life in a most undignified manner. For this eleven-year-old girl, it became a never-to-be forgotten, deeply humiliating memory.

Nevertheless, looking back on that experience much later, the thought of a missed bittersweet opportunity crossed my mind as I thought of Papa. I know what he would have had me do as a victorious parting act. At that poignant moment of urgency atop the mountain, had I been the boy that my father had so badly wanted, he would simply have had me unzip my pants, take careful aim northward, and with well-deserved gratification, relieve myself squarely in the face of the enemy--while yodeling at the top of my voice, "I piss on all of you-ou-ou-ou!"

But, the humor of such a triumphant final moment was lost on me at the time. For now, my pants were soaking wet, the night was still cold and windy, and there was a lot more walking to do. The inside of my wet pants soon began to freeze and chafe my thighs. I was visibly unhappy and, though he maintained tactful silence, my observant guide knew the reason.

We were going downhill now. The weather soon became less brutal. Then, as we went around a south-facing bend, I saw a few stars come into view in an otherwise gray-black sky. Still we walked. By now, the skin on the inside of my thighs was nearly raw and stung badly. Tears ran down my cheeks, as much from embarrassment as from the soreness now added to the fatigue I could hardly bear. I knew the guide was watching me so I tried not to walk bow-legged. But, every once in a while, an involuntary sob escaped my throat.

Once, in an effort to cheer me up, Monsieur Jean stopped me. The trail had opened up to reveal tiny points of light here and there in the black void beyond. He led me slightly off the trail.

"You see over there, where there's a faint halo of light on the horizon? That," he said, pointing southward toward a fuzzy gray area in the distance. "That's Barcelona. Your Maman and Papa are waiting there for you. You will see them in two or three days."

I was briefly overcome with joy. But when his words sank in, I became devastated. I had expected, and had counted on, being with my parents this very same day. I needed them desperately.

"Two or three days?" I looked at him in disbelief. "Nobody told me it would take two or three days after our crossing before I'd see them again."

I was heartbroken. Papa and Maman were so near, yet so far. My lips and chin quivered, and tears flowed again. Choking on new sobs, I cried openly.

"I thought they would come for us as soon as we crossed the border. Why are they still in Barcelona, why won't they come for us now?" I wailed.

Monsieur Jean put his hand gently on my shoulder, and led me back onto the path we had briefly left. "They cannot travel so close to the frontier." He explained gently. "There is too much risk of their being arrested by border guards and sent back to France."

He told me of the fragile nature of Spain's political neutrality at this time. Franco, Spain's relatively new dictator had struck several accords with Hitler. Not only were there large numbers of Jews fleeing Nazi persecution, there were also French political refugees, and men of military age trying to join DeGaulle's forces in England. Some accords required the arrest and return of political refugees to the Germans. Others demanded the return of Jews, like us, who had left without exit visas. These Jews were to be sent immediately to labor camps in Germany.

This was the most Monsieur Jean had spoken. In Barcelona, my parents were safe he said. We would be taken to them within a day or two after we reached our next destination. I wiped my eyes with my gloves and looked at him hoping things would come about just the way he explained. But I couldn't help wondering if there were any more surprises in store.

It was now pre-dawn Christmas day 1942.

CHAPTER XIII

¡Olé! ¡España!

Our first Spanish destination was in the general area of La Molina. How long a trek it was, I don't recall, but my raw inner thighs made sure I never forgot it. By the time we arrived at our next checkpoint, another shepherd hut, I had no choice but to walk bow-legged. Every step was utter torture.

By now, the sky had taken on a crepuscular deep steel blue color. Christmas day was about to dawn. A few lights twinkled brightly down in the Spanish lowlands and some shone here and there in the mountains as households stirred to greet the new day.

The hut we sought was like many other mountain huts I had seen since our arrival in Luchon. It was small but solidly constructed of stone and mortar, and had some ancillary structures nearby. Built to withstand the rough, bitter winters of the high mountains, it had heavy wooden doors, and its few windows were tightly shuttered against the cold. The main hut looked abandoned; there was no sign of life.

Nevertheless, we walked right in. A wave of warmth enveloped us immediately. Belying the impression it had given on the outside, the interior was aglow from several oil lamps, and a welcoming exuberant fire roared in the large hearth. Around it, several heavily dressed men sat talking quietly, sipping hot drinks from large mugs.

Some of our party had arrived earlier, so we were expected. In fact, Paulette had already been put to bed in a side room where Eveline would soon join her. Delicious warmth embraced my distressed muscles, and I felt myself starting to thaw.

A woman, dressed in several layers of hand-knitted gray woolens, came over to greet us. Her heavy sweater, coming halfway to her knees, concealed much of the long-sleeved dress she wore, and only the lowest parts of her stumpy legs covered in black stockings could be seen beneath a long skirt. Her slightly graying hair was pulled back in a bun, and she had the wizened appearance of people who live their entire lives in the mountains. Probably in her fifties, she looked much older.

Monsieur Jean exchanged a few words quietly with her in the customary *patois*, and a quick knowing glance was cast in my direction. Then he pushed me gently toward the woman.

"This is Señora Maria. She will take care of you and your sisters for the next day or two. Do exactly as she says." He also told me that her hut was as far as he could take us; he had to return to his French home right away.

Though I was emotionally and physically drained, I still felt a tightening in my throat at his words. This man of the mountains had rescued me from an icy grave. He had seen me at my best and at my worst, and he had comforted me when I needed it the most. We had begun to bond, he and I. Once again, I had to part with another of what I had cautiously begun to think of as a friend. [7]

Forlorn, I turned away from him and looked at my latest in a long list of surrogate mamans, another stranger who now offered me some sweetened hot milk. I took the mug she offered and numbly drank a little. Exhaustion had long ago replaced the hunger I had felt earlier in the night. Though she sat me down in front of a plate of hot food, I could not eat. I simply didn't have the strength to chew. On the verge of sleep, I put my head down on the table and closed my eyes.

---

7   He and I never said goodbye, and I never saw him again. I know that he and many others like him were paid well for smuggling Jews across the border. However, for many like him it was far more than a business arrangement. He and his mountain network put themselves at great risk every time they undertook another smuggling trek. They despised the Germans and what they represented. These treks were their way of fighting the enemy. I will always regret that I never had a chance to thank him properly for risking his life to save mine.

"*Pauvrrah petiteh.*" Poor little one, she said soothingly with the rolling accent I would hear many times from others in this region. She looked at me with understanding as she gently raised my head and tried to put a few spoonsful of stew in my mouth. It was futile. I no longer had the strength to swallow. Realizing sleep was what I needed most, she picked up an oil lamp, and partly carrying me, led me through a small covered breezeway into an attached cabin. This room was just big enough for a bed, a chest of drawers and a chair. But with no fireplace, there was no heat. I had literally stepped into an icebox.

The four-poster bed was hand-made of roughly hewn pine-like wood. Covering it were huge pillows and an enormous, billowy white *édredon* (eider down) quilt. I had never seen a duvet so light or puffed up so high before. I felt drawn to it like a magnet. I couldn't wait to crawl under it and wrap myself in its warm folds.

The woman brought my small suitcase with her and set it down at the foot of the bed. She told me to put on some warm dry clothes and get into bed quickly. I tried, but I couldn't undo my infernal belt knot so she had to help me with it. At last, I was free of the heavy wet wool between my legs that had felt like a hot metal rasp against my skin. My inner thighs were truly raw now; every move was accompanied by searing pain. Tears ran down my cheeks once again. With shaking hands, I struggled to put on my nightclothes. The woman, seeing my physical distress, said she wanted to bring me something and ran out.

In less than a minute, she was back with a mysterious pomade in hand. I was wretched when she applied it to my thighs but it did seem to ease the burning. Then, with teeth chattering, longing for that moment of sheer bliss that ushers in the sleep of total exhaustion, I crawled under the covers.

Icy cold, clammy sheets assaulted my body. The chattering of my teeth increased a notch, and my body began to shake violently. I whimpered, "I'm f-f-freezing." As she ran out, once more I heard the woman mutter, "*Pauvrrah petiteh.*"

Moments later she returned carrying hot bricks wrapped in thick towels, and a metal bed warmer. Gently, she placed the roll of bricks under the covers at the foot of the bed where my feet immediately and gratefully embraced them. The bed warmer, a long-handled, covered cast iron pan filled with hot coals followed. Telling me to move over to the opposite side and keep clear, she slowly passed it back and forth from the foot of the bed to the pillow. Still shaking, I rolled over while she "de-iced" the other side.

The entire bed was now exquisitely warm, and so soft and comforting that I immediately succumbed to sleep. What a deep sound sleep I had; I never heard the woman come in to check on me and replace the soiled garments of my misadventure with clean dry clothes. Thoughtfully, she placed them beneath the covers so they would be warm when I got up.

#

When I finally awoke, the cabin was dark. I had slept the entire day and part of the evening. I stretched luxuriously if cautiously. My thighs were considerably less painful now and I was starving. Having found my clothes with my toes, I quickly dressed between the sheets and ran into the main room. I was as eager to get away from the chill of my sleeping room as to get at the food.

My sisters had apparently been up for some time and were just finishing their supper. I joined them and ravenously ate everything that was put in front of me until I felt stuffed. Then, we were sent back to bed for more sleep.

At some point, well past midnight, we were wakened and prepared for travel once more. In the pre-dawn hours, we were piled into a mule cart and left the hut. Our destination, the woman said, was another rendezvous point a little further down the mountain.

With the rhythmic creaking and swaying of the cart and my hours of fear and crisis now behind me, I spent my time catching up on sleep. No longer did I feel the need to be alert or to pay attention to everything around me.

Our last relay point was Puigcerdà, a small border village near the railway line. We arrived there early in the morning. We ate. Then, after a short rest, we boarded an old local train for the final three or four hour leg to Barcelona.

#

The train wound its way slowly down the mountain. When it neared the Catalonia seaport, I impatiently craned my neck out the window; I needed reassurance so badly. Were Papa and Maman really still alive? Would they be at the station?

Then, as the train pulled in, I saw them grinning and waving wildly. At that first glimpse, indescribable relief washed over me and I thought my heart would burst with joy.

"Maman! Papa!" All three of us shouted wildly.

Our long, impatiently awaited family reunion was a tearful one. We could not hug and kiss each other enough. Absolute happiness filled my soul that whole day, as did hope: hope that in this neutral country there would be no more lies, no more hiding, no more being on guard all the time. There was comforting closure in my life. We were a whole family again with a chance at a new beginning.

#

Our sojourn in Barcelona was wonderful. What a beautiful city! I remember a broad avenue along which vendors hawked their wares, and where we strolled down to *la playa*, the beach. The weather was pleasant and the people were friendly. Though it had recently known the horrors of a civil war, Barcelona was now a city at peace.

Maman and Papa took us for long walks, as we used to do at home in Paris on Sunday afternoons so long ago--without needing to look over our shoulders. We would occasionally buy some coveted goodies when the family budget permitted;

this gave us the opportunity to practice our halting Spanish on vendors.

Maman's keen ear for languages helped her learn Spanish quickly. I guess I must have inherited a little of this native skill from her. I soon discovered Latin roots common to French and Spanish and relied on my creativity to bridge the two with what I picked up from my Barcelona playmates. Within three months, I was able to get by very well. Papa had a bit more trouble, so I became his interpreter when he went to the farmers' market or when we all went to street festivals.

I loved going to those fairs to stare bewitched at the dancers swirling passionately in brightly colored costumes. They reminded me so much of the gypsies of my earlier, carefree years. Some of the dancers were nearly my age and, in the lighthearted, ephemeral reality of street festivals, friendships were quickly made between us and as quickly forgotten.

So, for a short time the tightness eased that had been in my belly since the occupation of Luchon. Here, Nazi soldiers were not hunting "dirty Jews," I was reunited with my parents, and we could move about freely. It was exactly where I wanted to be.

If only time had stood still!

CHAPTER XIV

Adieu, Mes Amours

Barcelona, in a very short time, became a critical asylum for Jews. It was an important seaport, a center of lively economic activity with a good infrastructure, and it was the closest major city to the French border in the Pyrenees. Over the cols and snow-covered peaks of these mountains, thousands of Jews escaped from the certain death that awaited them at the hands of the Nazis. This accessible region became the only lifeline for our desperate people. Many escaped with nothing but the clothes on their backs, with no money or documents to prove their birthrights. They came as stateless illegals, in defiance of Nazi orders and without sponsors to pave the way.

Barcelona, therefore, was the ideal location for the Jewish Joint Distribution Committee, commonly known as "The Joint," to establish a "discreet" base of operations. Under the dedicated, skilled leadership of Dr. Samuel Sequerra, a Portuguese Jew who took over its operation in 1941, it successfully aided Jewish refugees for the duration of the war. This pivotal humanitarian organization quickly found my parents a modest home when they first arrived. A job for Papa also soon followed.

Amazingly, Franco--Spain's dictator--was willing to allow The Joint to feed, clothe, and house the beleaguered stream of Jews that came seeking refuge in his country. There was little or no cost to his struggling post-revolution economy since the funds to support this effort came from generous American Jews who gave millions of dollars for that purpose at a time when no one else would help.

A few refugees did manage to bring a little money with them. It was hidden in their clothing in the form of gold coins. I am certain my parents brought some gold with them too. My father would never have considered going to a foreign country without taking precautions against possible starvation. He was a man who always had a fallback plan. But, they could not possibly have survived the remainder of the war without some assistance from The Joint.

Dr. Schwartzbard, London's Polish Deputy Consul, remembered meeting Papa in Switzerland. He deputized him to assist with the displaced Jews of Poland who were able to make their way to Spain. It became Papa's responsibility, as a Polish national, to evaluate and process the large caseload of exiled Polish Jews who had fled their homes without proof of nationality. An office and a male secretary came with the job. As it turned out, this work kept him employed and safe in Barcelona until the end of hostilities with Germany.

However, in early 1943, the status of the war was very uncertain. Conditions changed almost daily. Rumors and speculation ran rampant. Within the Jewish community, there was mounting anxiety over events in North Africa. There was talk of a possible German offensive, through Spain, against the Allies who were now in Western North Africa. This would have brought Nazi troops down from France right into our midst once more. Papa and Maman talked about it constantly--and my anxiety returned.

#

One afternoon, Papa came home with pressing news.

"The Joint has arranged to transport Jewish refugee children to the United States," he announced excitedly to Maman.

"I think we should send the children. But we have to act quickly, because there is limited space."

He explained that this was a program being carried out with the help of at least two other American organizations: The American Friends Service Committee (AFSC), a Quaker aid group, and the Hebrew Immigrant Aid Society (HIAS). Yes, all three girls could go. Although it would cost the family several thousand francs toward our passage, Papa said it was worth it.

Furthermore, he had been given to understand that the parents of such children would be first to be granted United States entry visas when these coveted documents became available. No, he did not know how certain this was. So much depended on how the United States' quotas were prioritized. All he could say was that he was told negotiations were ongoing. But he believed the granting of such visas and the chances for a successful outcome were reasonably good.

Maman was stunned at first; then she was torn. I, for my part, was horrified. Papa was exhilarated. After all, it had been a lifelong dream of his to immigrate to the United States.

They discussed it candidly with me later that day. When I realized how convinced he was that this was the right thing to do, I burst into tears and begged him to keep us there with them. Our last separation was fresh in my mind and the anguish I had felt when I was hidden on the farm, away from my parents, was haunting me once more. "Why, Papa? Why do we have to leave you? I don't want to go. Why can't we stay together?"

I asked these questions over and over in the days that followed. He patiently and sadly tried to explain that Hitler was poised to move his troops into Spain. If this came to pass, we would have to run for our lives. He told me there were no more places left for Jews to run in Europe. With three small children along, it would be almost impossible to flee or hide. In such case, it would put all of us at great risk. No, we could not all stay together. There was too much uncertainty, too much danger. In America, we would be safe, and he tried to assure me it would probably not be too long before we would all be together again.

I kept protesting. I begged Maman and then I begged Papa. I desperately wanted to remain with my parents no matter what the danger, uncertainty or circumstances. I didn't care; I wanted to be with my parents. But Papa was resolute and Maman was resigned. I, on the other hand, was angry: at the Nazis, at my parents and at my helplessness.

We filled out applications and began to prepare for the trip. Appropriate documents were filed, and visa photos were taken. The processing went through amazingly fast, and all too soon, the required travel documents were ready.

Our visas were issued on March 24, 1943.

#

Maman lovingly stitched little name labels inside all of the clothing we were to take with us. Though she was heavyhearted herself, she used every trick she knew to get me excited over the coming voyage. She called it our great adventure and enthused about all the interesting sights I was going to see. She talked of the relatives we were going to meet, such as her brother Harry in Philadelphia with whom she said we might be going to live. Papa's cousin, Maurice Coel, was in New York City where I would see the Statue of Liberty. And I would make many new friends on the boat and in our new country.

But, still, I cried. At such times, Maman cradled me in her arms and, in her lovely voice, sang to me a melancholy French song about one's love departing one day on a boat to a far-away place. It only made us both cry that much more.

After a while, however, I did allow myself to be swept into the excitement of the promised adventure that lay ahead. I was titillated at the prospect of meeting other children like me and making new friends. It had been too dangerous to talk openly about my religion, or to invite anyone to our home to play. Avoiding social interaction altogether had been much easier, so I had become accustomed to solitary activities. This pattern of behavior lingered. I had learned to depend on myself for entertainment.

Yes, Maman was probably right. The trip could be a carefree opportunity to make new friends. But I rarely thought very long about such things without coming right back to the approaching breakup of our family, and my heart ached more with each passing day.

I could see that Maman's heart was heavy too. She was so pale, and she sighed often and so deeply. I guessed she must have been having many sleepless nights.

A day or two before our departure, while Papa was out on an errand, Maman and I had a serious conversation about how different our lives would be after we left. She told me I would soon become very important to my sisters, and that I should talk to them often about their parents so they would not forget them. She was counting on me to be a good role model and take good care of them too.

"You must watch over them, don't let anything happen to them."

"But, Maman," I asked. "How am I going to know what to do? I'm a little girl. I don't know how to take care of children."

This assertion must have touched a raw nerve; it brought Maman close to tears. She took me in her arms and hugged me so tightly that I could hardly breathe. After a long pause, she put me at arm's length, looked at me solemnly and took a deep breath. Then, she spoke.

"Jacqueline, *mon amour.* You must give me your word ..." And in the next few moments, my life was redefined. She asked me to take "the dreaded oath." "You must swear ..."

The die was cast. I had no choice. I swore as my mother asked, never to allow anything to happen to my sisters ... lest "God strike me dead!"

That night, I lay awake for hours going over everything imaginable that might possibly happen to my siblings. I tried to sort out all the "what ifs" of my future as a child-parent--without parents of my own to turn to for guidance. The possibilities seemed endless and terribly frightening. That night, the first of many to come, I cried myself to sleep.

#

Time passed too quickly. One morning in early April 1943, we rose and dressed in silence while Papa and Maman took care of final preparations for our voyage. That afternoon, we were to meet our chaperones and the rest of the children in our convoy. I could tell Maman had been crying. Her eyes were red and swollen; her skin, now pale, made the dark circles under her eyes even more noticeable. As for Papa, he was unusually quiet.

We ate our breakfasts without a word. Afterwards, Papa pulled me aside. Taking my face in his hands he said, "*Jacquot Chérie,* you must promise me one thing. You must write to us every week and tell us all the things that you and your sisters have done." He paused for a moment. "Swear, *Chérie,* that you will do this."

I looked at my father. He knew how much I detested writing letters. He wasn't so fond of it himself. Resentment had already begun to fester inside of me about this whole unwanted departure and about the mounting responsibilities I was being given. Deep down, I placed a certain amount of blame on my father for what was coming to pass.

Now, he was asking me to take on one more unwanted task! But there was no arguing with Papa. So, another vow was extracted from me, and another grown-up responsibility was placed on my shoulders.

#

At the orientation meeting that afternoon, we learned that we three were among a small few who were not war orphans. The age range was four to sixteen. We were told that ours was the third convoy of Jewish children being rescued in 1943. Three others were to follow ours that year. An informal consortium of dedicated volunteers and organizations had joined forces to make this all come about.

The International Red Cross, The Joint, The American Friends Service Committee, and Hebrew Immigrant Aid Society among others were working together to bring hidden and displaced children safely out of Nazi-occupied Europe. Judging from the languages they spoke, most of the children who were there that day came from central and Eastern Europe. Many were bound for the United States, sponsored by Eleanor Roosevelt's U.S. Committee for the Care of European Children (USCCEC). Others would go to countries such as Chile and Canada. (The name of the committee did not reflect its true purpose: the rescue of Jewish children. Its real purpose had to be veiled in order to protect the Roosevelt administration from political repercussions by right-wing Nazi sympathizers in the United States who did not want foreign Jews brought to the United States.)

Names were called from a roster. A few did not respond; they were still en route from wherever they had been hidden. We were organized into age groups, and each one had its own assigned chaperone. My first reaction was one of panic; my sisters were not in my group! I immediately took charge. After all, they were my responsibility now. With some fear of being refused, I approached the group leader with my request, "I want my sisters with me all the time please!"

Most of the thirty-some children in this convoy were without siblings. Such a question had not previously been raised. But the staff was extremely sensitive to our needs. Since I was the only one with two siblings in this convoy, they were willing to make an exception. We were set up as a separate group of three--at least for the train trip.

I had taken the first step in my new role.

Each child in the group was assigned a code number to be used later for reassembling at the train station, and each of us was given an identification tag to pin onto our coat lapel. On it was our name, group code, and chaperone. We were also given similarly labeled little satchels for a few personal effects such as toothbrush, toothpaste, hairbrush and photos of loved ones. Instructions were given, and after a question and answer period, we were told where and when to report that evening at the train station for the overnight trip to Madrid. Then, we were dismissed--for our final family afternoon together in Barcelona.

#

At the train station that evening, there we stood, three little girls--eleven, six and four years of age--waiting with our small bags of clothing at our sides, frightened and forlorn. Our identification tags had carefully been pinned to our coat lapels by Maman, who had wept most of the afternoon.

I looked over anxiously at my parents, a short distance away. They were talking quietly to our chaperone. They glanced at me several times as I clutched my sisters' hands.

Other children could also be seen gathered in small clusters around certain adults--some, holding signs. All of us were waiting for the train that would change our lives in ways none could foresee.

#

While I waited for the "All aboard," a haunting sense of destiny stirred in my heart. I was to leave one world of uncertainty for another far from the parents I loved and far from the life, language, and culture I knew. All that was familiar and dearest to my heart, I was soon to leave behind. I kept wondering how old I would be when--or if--I would see my maman and papa again.

Getting all the children organized with their assigned chaperones and on board in their proper compartments took a long time. When at last we were on board, I lowered our car window and clutched at the outreached hands of Maman and Papa and the comforting squeezes that I knew would come from them. We spoke lovingly to each other, and I held back my tears for I had promised myself to be very brave. I had begun to take some measure of comfort in thinking that the train might never leave when the warning whistle finally sounded. It startled me and a chill went down my spine. The inevitability of our departure was at hand; I could not stop the march of time. Despite my resolve, my tears now overflowed.

The scene that followed had a dreamlike quality. Vividly etched in my memory and replayed hundreds of times in my head over the years, it returns occasionally to haunt me. That same sense of powerlessness, of disbelief returns as, again and again, I see the train begin to ease forward. As it moves, I am still holding Maman's hands. Then the train picks up a little speed; I can no longer hold on to her hands. More whistles sound. My heart beats fast. I crane my neck through the car window with my head toward the platform to get a last look at my cherished parents, to fix their faces in my mind for always as the train pulls away from the station.

Dozens of other little hands like mine reach out through open windows. The crowd on the platform follows alongside the moving train, unhurriedly at first, then faster and faster to keep up. The futile chase is abandoned slowly, except for one lone tearful woman. She is running alongside the train, unwilling to give up. When the end of the platform is reached, she finally stops, unable to go further.

It is my Maman.

For a long time I stare out of the train window, sobbing, choking on the heavy lump in my throat. Is this truly happening? This must be a bad dream. Am I really leaving my home, my family and my history for good? Will I ever see my parents again?

I sense an unsettling lurch forward in the karma of my destiny. A strange, surreal feeling suddenly overcomes me and a disquieting sensation of finality takes its place. In that moment, I remember my little sisters and turn around.

Four-year-old Paulette and six-year-old Eveline are huddled together on their seats clinging to one another, crying because they see me cry. A new chill runs down my spine. In this sobering moment of transition, choking on my sobs, I confront squarely the reality of my new role in life and my tears stop.

I wrap my arms around my little sisters and hug them, oh so tight. I must be their new source of comfort now, their new Maman.

CHASED BY DEMONS

PART FIVE

WHAT WAS FOUND

CHAPTER XV

Mainsail West!

At least three Red Cross nurses chaperoned our group. Ours sat down with us shortly after our train left Barcelona to reassure us that we would never be alone. "One of us will be with you the entire time." Good, I thought. Eveline and Paulette won't be able to stray too far from the main group during the train ride. Since our chaperone spoke Spanish as well as our own tongue, she said she would also act as our interpreter. I must have had an anxious look on my face for she stopped briefly and looked at me. "Do you have any questions?"

"Yes!" A thought had popped into my head prompted by a familiar pressure starting to build inside the lower part of my torso. "What if one of my sisters needs to go pipi? Who will take her to the bathroom?"

The chaperone smiled knowingly. "You may take her if you like, as long as you ask me or one of the other chaperones before you go." And she showed me where the narrow door was to a tiny bathroom at the end of our car, with a warning about not letting anything of value drop into the toilet as it would fall right out onto the tracks and never be seen again.

At the thought of the open hole, I felt my urge receding.

"Where are we going?" I pressed further, wanting to change the subject.

"Our final destination is Lisboa, Portugal, where you will board your ship. But, we will stop in Madrid first to pick up more children tomorrow."

When I asked how far it was, she said it was some four hundred miles from Barcelona. "It will take all night; so we have to sleep on the train."

While the train took us farther and farther away from our loved ones, she reviewed the rules of conduct we were to follow en route and reminded us that, under no circumstances were we to remove the identification tags we had on our outer garments. She also went over the procedures that we were to follow when we arrived at the Madrid and Lisbon train stations. Each of us had assigned partners whose hand we were to hold onto, and we were to stay right behind our chaperone until we were told otherwise.

Almost as if she could read my mind, she said, "Don't worry, Jacqueline. No one will be left behind." and she patted my hand. "Your little sisters will be your assigned partners."

I listened intently to every word she said and slowly I began to feel less vulnerable. It seemed the Red Cross had thought of everything; contrary to my original conviction, I would not have to face the world alone.

#

Our arrival Sunday morning in Madrid went without incident. A bus was waiting to take us to the Hotel Mediodía where we had lunch. This was followed by routine announcements; then we were sent to our rooms for a nap until our train departure for Lisbon. While we rested, eight additional children joined the group. Then, we were on our way again.

When we reached our Lisbon destination, the Portuguese Red Cross took over. They told us the sailing date had not yet been confirmed, so it wasn't known exactly when we would be boarding our ship.

Housing was waiting for us. Arrangements had been made through the *Assistencia Publica*. The boys went to a boys' school in Lisbon, and we girls went to the *Colonia de Repouso da Educação Popular*, a school farther up in the hills. This school was next to a convent on a slope that overlooked the port of Lisbon, close to Estoril. From there, I could, just barely, see the harbor. I looked in that direction often, hoping to catch sight of our ship, but with the many ships anchored there, it was futile to try.

Sisters of Charity in their blue frocks, and with pointed white starched headdresses that cast long shadows over their faces, hosted our stay. Gracious and sensitive, they respected our ethnicity; Catholic prayers were never imposed on us.

Each of us was assigned to a dormitory as soon as we arrived. Though spartan, our room was large, very clean and comfortable enough. As for our meals, though they did not measure up to my Maman's creative standards, they were, nevertheless, tasty and adequate.

Every morning during our stay, the Sisters sent us out into the courtyard and had us play active games. Physical conditioning was something we all needed. Many of us had been living sedentary lives indoors, while in hiding. Our growing bodies had been deprived of the kinds of activities necessary for normal development. The games we were encouraged to play helped build up our bodies for the upcoming long days at sea as well. For me, this passage with the Sisters of Charity--in contrast to my previous convent experience--was a pleasant, almost healing one.

I found Portugal beautiful. A brilliant mid-April sun shone every day, and the hillsides, with their dazzling whitewashed buildings scattered here and there, sparkled against clear blue skies. This was a world at peace. Seagulls--not bombers-- flew overhead. I felt joyful. Spring was around the corner and anticipation of a fresh start was everywhere. The days ahead held some element of promise and, yes, exciting adventure as well. Although our future was still uncertain, there was now reason for hope.

#

Toward the end of our week's stay in Lisbon, five other children joined us. At final count, there were thirty-five Jewish refugee children. Some were from cities or towns in central

Europe where ongoing underground efforts had made their escape possible. They had found their way to Spain and, with The Joint's help, had been able to qualify for our convoy. All were under sixteen, in keeping with the USCCEC's age requirements. At the last minute, the Committee had expedited the processing of their entry visas in Madrid; this was the only official American assistance offered to Jews whose lives now depended wholly on the United States.

HIAS, The Joint, and the Quakers' AFSC made the last minute arrangements for necessary departure documents and ship's clearances. There had been several delays and changes of dates while we, the ship's special cargo, waited with mixed feelings of anticipation, apprehension and heartache.

#

Shortly before our departure from Lisbon, the boys were brought to our school by bus. That morning, we were told of their estimated arrival time so, after breakfast, I went to an upstairs window that faced the harbor below to watch for their arrival. My patience was soon rewarded when I saw their bus snaking up the hill between rows of red tiled roofs. Slowly it negotiated each switchback curve until it finally pulled up in front of our school. By this time, all of us girls were pressed against the front gate, eager to see our travel mates again and to check out the new arrivals. The boys piled out, all jabbering something about an interview.

Sure enough, a radio crew from a local broadcasting station had followed the bus and arrived a few minutes later. Apparently, we were newsworthy! Everyone was excited over this unexpected event, especially after the staff told us we'd have a chance to say a few words into the microphone to loved ones. How exciting. We were going to be on the radio!

Like flies, we swarmed around the newscaster, squealing for attention and jockeying to gain the best possible position for a chance at the microphone. Everyone wanted to be first. Upon a given sign by the engineer, we all fell silent.

After a few introductory remarks in Portuguese by the radio host, it was our turn. "Speak clearly." We were told. Suddenly, a microphone was thrust in my face. My big moment of celebrity was at hand.

Shyly I gave my name and where I was born, *"Je m'appelle Jacqueline Grossman et je suis française."* I said with pride. It felt so good to be able to give my real name without fearing the consequences of revealing I was Jewish.

Slowly and succinctly, as we had been instructed, I started my message to my parents. I had prepared it in my head and I wanted them to hear every word. *"Bonjour, Maman et Papa.* We arrived safely and we are waiting in Lisboa to get on the boat. I miss you a lot and I..."

Just then, the microphone was whisked away from my face to be thrust into that of another. I guess I must have taken longer than time permitted. The radio host obviously spoke no French and did not understand how important my final words were. I tried to explain to him that I had not finished saying, *"Je vous aime,* (I love you)." to my parents. But he just ignored me and went on to the others. I was heartbroken.

#

Our embarkation day, April 17, 1943, finally arrived. With mixed feelings we boarded the SS Serpa Pinto. I was ambivalent; I liked Portugal and I was still on the same continent with Papa and Maman. This little connection to my parents was important to me and I wouldn't have minded remaining right there. On the other hand, I was getting tired of the regimentation; I couldn't go off exploring on my own, and I was eager to meet my uncle, Harry Gelsman, in the United States.

Finally, passengers and cargo were loaded and the ship was ready. As it pulled away from the pier, the same kind of strange

surreal feeling that I had experienced on the train when I left
Barcelona revisited me. I stood at the railing with tears running
down my face while the unseen arms of my longing heart reached
out toward the disappearing coastline to touch my Maman and
Papa one last time. Oh, how I missed them!

When the coast of Portugal could no longer be seen on the
horizon, we knew warring Europe was now behind us. An
announcement on the loud speaker told us to go below; there
was business to be addressed. We all gathered together for our
orientation and instructions. My sisters and I were assigned our
sleeping quarters. I didn't have to worry about the girls because
our cabin was next to that of our chaperones. I knew they would
be closely supervised. Besides, there were recreational activities
planned for the youngest ones by the staff for every day we were
at sea.

The walls on each side of our small cabin were lined with
several narrow bunks. The tallest of us were assigned the top
bunks. The youngest got the beds below. Lighting was dim
below deck in these inside cabins and space was cramped. I had
always loved light and space; it was depressing for me to stay
down there for very long. Therefore, as soon as I got up and
dressed in the morning, I left my quarters and stayed on deck as
much as possible. With Eveline and Paulette in the care of the
chaperones, I knew I didn't have to worry too much about them.

The Serpa Pinto was a small steamship. She had been a
valiant veteran of seagoing refugee service since 1940. This
was her third year. Her crew knew what their cargo was about.
They had hosted other similar transports and showed no hint of
prejudice because we were Jews.

In fact, they were very friendly, despite the fact that--
according to what we had been told by our chaperones--they
had orders from their captain to keep their minds on their work
and not fraternize with us. We came to know many of them on a
personal level and made the most of our all-too-brief friendships
with them. We asked a lot of questions about their homes and

tried to learn a little Portuguese from them. Some of them even showed us how to make those intricate knots that every sailor has to know. How proud they were of their skill. When we ran out of questions, we found other ways to pass the time.

The Serpa Pinto's seamen wore what we thought were funny naval caps with green pompons on top. These pompons became tempting targets. Teasing and harmless pre-teen flirtations with cute young sailors (many of them still in their teens) followed. One game the girls loved to play required sneaking up on a sailor from behind and jumping up to touch his cap's pompon without his being aware he had been a target. Then we'd run away and hide. Our reward for being successful was supposedly a streak of good luck. If unsuccessful, we got a not too serious rebuke from a cute sailor. Although embarrassment could not be avoided, the end result was actually welcomed; the girlish banter that followed with the sailor was its own reward--followed by lots of giggles from all of us.

The boys in our convoy took part on the side. They placed bets on which girls would succeed, all the while poking fun at us. Sometimes, while we slithered near our "prey," their antics gave us away; the target sailor would turn around to catch us in the act, and we'd lose that round. Everyone enjoyed these diversions during the long and boring days at sea, including the young sailors.

The voyage was relatively uneventful except for occasional alerts of submarines nearby. At such times, there was a sudden flurry of activity. Both crew and passengers scurried for life preservers and designated lifeboat stations, where we remained until after the all clear was announced. Although the SS Serpa Pinto flew the flag of a neutral country, it didn't prevent our being scoped, and we worried about torpedoes being accidentally or deliberately released.

Danger was very real from above as well. Axis planes flew overhead to check us out a few times. Fortunately, nothing came of these occurrences, except for some serious tightening of our stomachs and a lot of racing pulses. [8]

Nature also made its contribution to our discomfort. In April, the seas are often rough. The Serpa Pinto was not a luxury liner; its primary use in peacetime had been short crossings of passengers, or long distance merchant shipping. We jokingly referred to the Serpa Pinto as the Banana Boat. She had originally been built as a merchant ship in 1914 and had been sold several times before becoming the SS Serpa Pinto of a Lisbon company in 1940. She was not equipped with the kinds of stabilizers often found on large passenger vessels or on ships of younger vintage.

Many passengers, children and adults alike, were seasick. I was fortunately not plagued by this condition, but my little sisters were not so lucky. On more than one occasion, I had to ask for the group's doctor to give them something for relief. But there was little relief to be had from the lingering stench of sour vomit below--another reason not to remain there any longer than necessary. Besides, the other young passengers of my age were above on deck most of the time. That's where all the fun and socializing went on.

With the weight of responsibility for two little ones and no other family here in my life, making new friends suddenly became very important to me. I needed a buddy. I needed someone to whom I could pour out my heart; I needed someone with whom mutually shared thoughts could be a source of comfort for both, without becoming overly dependent on each other. I needed

---

8 A year later, during another of her humanitarian crossings, the SS Serpa Pinto was not quite so lucky. She was stopped by gunfire from a surfaced U-boat and was boarded by its captain who threatened to torpedo her. The Portuguese captain, expecting the worst, gave an "Abandon Ship" order unaware that Berlin had sent a last minute message to the German captain countermanding his actions. The SS Serpa Pinto was then permitted to proceed. Before this occurred, however, two passengers had immediately gone overboard upon hearing the Portuguese order to abandon ship; tragically, they could not later be found. One of the missing was an infant.

someone close who, unlike my sisters, would not be another responsibility, would not be a burden. I also hungered for friendships with "my own kind." It had been a long time since I had been able to be my real self, totally open, simply a child without adult secrets. I ached for carefree companionship and affection.

Now, suddenly, children were all around me from whom I did not have to hide, to whom I did not have to lie. All at once, there was so much freedom: to play openly, to live, and to simply be a child without parental supervision or discipline. It was like being at summer camp, or taking a deep breath of fresh air.

So, with three months' worth of broken street Catalan Spanish, fluent French, enough Yiddish to break the ice, and with the ingenuity all children have, I hungrily seized the opportunity to seek new friends. I plunged in.

But, I soon learned it wasn't going to be easy. There were too many different languages. Besides France, these children came from Austria, Belgium, Poland, Germany, Bessarabia, and Yugoslavia. Their languages were different from the ones I had heard at home. Furthermore, few of them spoke Yiddish. My parents had deliberately helped me learn the rudiments of it in Barcelona so I could communicate with my Polish uncle in America. Then, there were the age differences. As small a gap as six months in birth dates was important at eleven years of age.

It had never occurred to me that making friends would be difficult. Also, more important than language or age was culture. Some children perceived themselves to be of higher social status. They possibly came from former wealthy, prominent families in central Europe. This was reflected in their attitudes and created a palpable social barrier. These children remained distant and cliquish. Some of the older ones even exhibited a familiar arrogance, the kind I identified with the German culture. They ironically reminded me of the Nazi world I had left behind. I instinctively shied away from them.

However, there were others who, like me, were open to being friends. We became intensely close. There was one in particular, a boy about my age, whose story was very sad; he had lost his family. We did not connect until later in the voyage. But when we did, a close rapport developed quickly. He spoke French. We talked about many things, about ourselves, about the War, about the new country that would soon be our next home. Talking together was very comforting. We exchanged heartaches of the past and our hopes for the future.

He was alone, bound for a city somewhere in the interior, possibly Detroit, where he had relatives. His name may have been Harman or Armand. I have long regretted that this brief youthful friendship of ours did not have a chance to grow and mature into a lifelong one in the United States. We did not realize that, once in America, our departures from one another would be abrupt and final. We were all bound for various destinations in our new land, never to see each other again, another heartbreak in a seemingly endless stream of heartbreaks.

Nevertheless, for a fleeting moment in time, we all found solace and affection as well as companionship with each other. We had common backgrounds. We were children who had grown old before our time. We had all been vilified, persecuted, traumatized, and chased out of our homelands by a power-hungry madman. But we were resilient, and we now had a new chance at life.

#

I had looked forward with much anticipation to seeing the Statue of Liberty on our way into New York. From my history classes, I knew that it had been a gift to the United States from my own country. I was taught that it was given as a symbol of hope and liberty. How ironic, I thought, that in the very land of my birth, by Vichy France's heinous policies and decrees, my own hope and liberty had been deliberately, and with malice, taken away.

Sadly, this monument's symbolic flame of hope did not light our way into port. The Serpa Pinto had to be re-routed to Philadelphia. We were told the waters of the New York Harbor had been mined to protect the seaport from possible enemy submarine activity. Those waters could no longer be safely navigated. So it was the waterfront of Philadelphia's inland port that gave us our first view of the United States. To be honest, most of us were more than slightly disappointed. None of the glamour that we had expected was there to greet us.

Nevertheless, on April 30, 1943, with much hope and nervous excitement, we pressed ourselves against the railing to watch with awe as our ship slowly made its way through the busy harbor. The crew was in full dress uniform; the passengers wore their cleanest clothes. Big smiles lit up all our faces. The air was filled with intoxicating anticipation. We scrutinized everything in sight and waved at anything that moved. Signs of economic health and industry were everywhere. Best of all, there were no bombed buildings.

For a couple of hours, we continued at a snail's pace along this busy waterway. As usual, I was impatient. I asked myself a million questions as I scanned forward and aft. When are we going to dock? How far down this inlet do we have to go? It's so narrow. Oops! That was close. Where did that little boat come from? Does the Captain really know what he's doing?

At long last, we slid alongside our pier, quietly and without fanfare. After nearly two weeks, the SS Serpa Pinto finally turned off its engines. Compared to the helter skelter activities of all the docks we had passed, ours seemed very quiet, as if it were trying to hide. Dockhands were moving about as usual, but otherwise, very few people were there. To my knowledge, except for a telegram sent to their Philadelphia headquarters by the American Friends' field office in Lisbon confirming the names of passengers making the crossing, no acknowledgment-- official or otherwise--was made of our arrival.

We were certainly newsworthy but publicity for this event was deliberately avoided. The last thing the Roosevelt administration wanted was an embarrassing announcement of new Jewish refugee arrivals when right wing factions were set against bringing Jewish refugees to the United States. There was no press, no fuss, and no cameras.

Nevertheless, what a thrilling moment it was to watch the land-based gangway slowly edge up, the first American object was going to touch our ship. It felt as though unseen arms had reached across to enfold us in a warm embrace and whispered a comforting, "Welcome home. You're safe now!"

We displaced children of the world's most unwanted people were about to step onto American soil. When the gangway set down, a loud cheer went up.

CHAPTER XVI

The New World

As soon as the gangway was secured, a Port Authority official came aboard. Passenger manifests and cargo inventories were checked. Then, we had to be processed and approved by U.S. Immigration and representatives of health agencies. Only then, could we be turned over to our sponsors.

I watched the health officers make their way up the gangway with a little trepidation. The previous officials who had come on board had looked at 'things'. This group was going to look at people, at us! Would we be allowed to stay? Or, would we be sent back? Many of us had asked each other these questions while we were still on the open seas. During the voyage, I had often thought about the day I would walk off the ship to take my first step on the American continent, safe at last. I had imagined myself being the first one to run down the gangway and had packed my bag early. I was ready to go. I hoped and prayed with all my heart that we would pass the health inspection.

Though we were apparently all right, the Grossman girls did not get off the ship that day, or the day after. Not long after these initial formalities were addressed, I began to have the feeling that our voyage was to end differently from what I had expected.

Those of us whose relatives or sponsors were already committed to providing homes for them were reasonably secure. Their sponsors came one after another within the first day or two following our arrival in Philadelphia to claim their wards. I watched several of my new friends leave with their meager belongings, to be greeted somewhat stiffly at first by near-strangers willing to open their homes and hearts to them. I watched them go, one by one, and wondered dejectedly when or if I would ever see any of them again.

Time wore on; we waited.

Maman had told me that Uncle Harry, the eldest of her siblings, was our sponsor. Although it was not yet certain, she had hoped we might go live with him. So I was not surprised, a day or two later, to be told by our chaperone that he was to come aboard. I ran to the gangway, my sisters right behind me, and looked out eagerly onto the dock below, scanning the people who were gathered there, as I went. A woman in a small group was pointing in my direction.

Suddenly, there he was. A short stocky man with a vaguely familiar look started walking up the gangway. He was alone without his American wife, Aunt Caroline. We had never met before, although I had seen some old pictures of him.

He approached me, "Jacqueline?"

I nodded, smiling shyly.

"*Ich bin dein Mama's bruder*, Hahrry." He introduced himself in Yiddish.

I did the same and extended my hand in the French manner as was done at home when meeting someone for the first time. He shook my hand but went a step further and pulled me into his arms to give me a big bear hug. I felt awkward because I didn't really know him. In France, our ways were very formal; we didn't hug people we didn't know. But I was glad that he wanted to. I promptly introduced my sisters, who were with me now at all times. He hugged them as well and gave each of us candy bars as welcoming presents. I, in turn, gave him the letter that Maman had written to him in Yiddish and that she had entrusted to my care before we left. He read it eagerly, and I saw tears fill his eyes.

We talked for some time. It was good to be able to communicate directly without an interpreter to superimpose shades of meaning. I had wondered if we would be able to understand each other. He told me all about my three cousins, his sons, Arthur, Eugene and Norman. Cousins had always meant close friendships and fun times. I was excited at the prospect of meeting them and became even more impatient to leave the ship.

"Are we going to go to your home now?" I asked eagerly at the first tactful opportunity.

"No, not yet. There are some questions that still need to be addressed. I can't say for sure if we'll be able to have you come live with us." He looked uneasy.

I wasn't prepared for that answer. For a moment, I was speechless. I felt dejected as well as rejected. All kinds of thoughts went through my mind. Why can't he say? Who will take care of us if he can't? Maybe he doesn't like us.

I looked at him to evaluate him as a surrogate father. I needed to wash away my disappointment, so I said to myself, he's all right but I'm not sure I want to live with him anyway. Among other things, I noticed he had a builder's rough hands and I was accustomed to Papa's smooth, manicured ones. But when I remembered his sons, my new cousins, I was disappointed all over again. I really did want to get to know them.

Our visit concluded not long after his surprise announcement. Uncle Harry promised to come back soon. Oh, yes! Please come back! Even though I was a bit angry with him for not taking us off the ship that very day, I did want to see him again. By now, I had come to look upon the Serpa Pinto as a kind of prison. I was fearful that the longer we stayed aboard, the greater the chances were that we would have to sail back across the Atlantic with her. Was I never going to get off this infernal ship?

Uncle Harry kept his promise and returned the next day. This time, he did take us off the ship but only for a short visit near the dock. How thrilled I was to take that very first step on the American continent! I did it! I really did it, I said to myself in awe of the milestone it represented.

But the news my uncle brought dimmed the glow of that moment.

"I won't be able to have you and your sisters come live with us."

I was stunned. I had so counted on my uncle giving me guidance with my oath. Now, what was I going to do?

"*Ober far vos?*" "But why?" I asked. " Maman told me that we ..."

As if he didn't want me to finish the sentence, he interrupted to explain that Aunt Caroline's health was not good. She was unable to care for three young children. She had three boys of her own. Apparently her heart was not strong.

"But you will not be sent back to Spain. Arrangements are being made for you to remain in America."

#

Several mornings after our arrival in the port of Philadelphia, we, the last three refugee children from Paris via Vierzon, Toulouse, Luchon, Barcelona, and Lisbon, finally disembarked the SS Serpa Pinto. A new chaperone, a caseworker from the European Jewish Children's Aid agency, was now in charge of our care.

We had lived in small, cramped ship's quarters for three weeks. Once again, all three of us were infested with lice. To make matter worse, we also had scabies. The treatment of these conditions was the first order of business in our new land. So, we were taken by local train to an agency infirmary.

The building was old and its corridors were dark. Glossy beige paint with brown wainscoting covered the interior walls. Ancient radiators clicked as they heated the high-ceilinged hallways. The odor of countless coats of enamel paint filled my nostrils. Combined with the smells of ether and other medicines, the air was sickeningly heavy and reminded me of my last visit to a French clinic.

After a long wait on hard benches outside an office, we were admitted into the treatment center and examined by medical staff. Immediate treatment was ordered.

In a short while, we were stripped and put into deep bathtubs filled with a blue therapeutic solution, the first of several treatments that would rid us of our unwanted guests. Apparently, we were potential walking epidemics.

We remained in this infirmary a few days while our nit-infested clothes were destroyed and new ones issued, our conditions further evaluated and treated, and our final dossiers completed. During this time, decisions regarding our disposition were also finalized. We were to be placed in the care of the Jewish Children's Bureau of Cleveland, a sub-agency of the Jewish Family Service there. That is how Cleveland, Ohio became our new home.

Sadly, Cleveland was too far from Philadelphia and from my uncle to foster the bonding of family that Maman had hoped would come about. Fate had clearly not intended for us to be raised by my mother's brother, an ironic note on the City of Brotherly Love.

Instead, and since my parents were unable to send money for our care, we became wards of a charitable Jewish agency in Cleveland. We remained there, on welfare, for over four years.

#

When we arrived in Cleveland, we were taken directly to the Bellefaire Jewish Orphan Home where we registered on June 2, 1943. No one spoke French there; and although they were all Jews like us, very few of the staff spoke Yiddish. I felt totally isolated; a buffer of silence suddenly surrounded me. I imagined this was how life might be on the moon, heavy stillness everywhere and no sounds at all. I couldn't interact with other children. I couldn't ask questions. I couldn't understand instructions. Neither could I express my needs, physical or emotional.

English had no common roots with French, as had been the case with Spanish. I couldn't even begin to guess at the meanings of the strange mouthings so totally foreign to my ears. I felt abandoned and painfully lonely. Having to look after my little sisters only heightened my sense of isolation and loneliness.

Since they couldn't communicate either, I worried about them all the time. Were they able to convey their needs to the cottage mother? My oath pressed on my mind.

On the positive side, the setting of the orphanage, on the outskirts of the city, was lovely, almost pastoral. Neat manicured expanses of tree-lined lawns were everywhere. A beautiful octagon-shaped chapel stood in the center of the peaceful campus. We were housed in cottages that included living, eating, and sleeping accommodations. All such dormitory cottages were arranged in a large circle around the chapel.

Our home cottage was assigned to us by sex and age. Each one housed eighteen children who were supervised by a resident "cottage mother." Boys were on one side of the campus, girls on the other. At one pole, between these two major groups of cottages, were a nursery, laundry, and dispensary; at the other, was the administration building. All of Bellefaire's structures were made of red brick with wood trim painted white.

My sisters were housed together in the same cottage with the other young children, as I had requested. Fearing that they might need my help, I looked in on them frequently, but they adapted quickly.

As for me, there were lots of surprises in store. My first breakfast at Bellefaire was an unforgettable experience. One long table had been set up with eighteen bowls and spoons. In the center of this table were several aluminum pitchers filled with orange juice, milk and hot chocolate, a few sugar bowls and some tall, slim open cardboard boxes with colorful pictures on them. As soon as our cottage mother sat down--and following her daily announcements--the girls all reached for these boxes at once and poured some contents into their bowls. Not wanting to appear dumb, I followed their example and did likewise and, as they did, I poured milk over it. My first mouthful caused me to choke. I didn't know how to deal with the little pieces that, to me, felt and tasted like thin chunks of cardboard. I had never been introduced to dry cereal before. I thought longingly of the tasty breakfast Maman always gave us.

In that former life, breakfast had consisted of a long piece of crusty French bread spread with butter, that I dipped into a big bowl of hot chocolate or very light café-au-lait before placing the tasty drippy morsel in my eager mouth. Sometimes, I also had a soft-boiled egg. In Spain and Portugal, there had been slight variations. But never, ever had I been expected to eat cardboard! And more surprises were yet to come in this unexpected collision of cultures.

When I was first introduced to my cottage mates, they were very interested in me; I did not speak their language. Contrary to my experiences, this was their first exposure to a foreigner, one who spoke no English. Our cottage mother urged them to teach me English and try to learn some French words from me at the same time.

For the first day or two, this seemed to break the ice a little. We all gesticulated crazily as if we were playing a game of charades, and for a time, these antics were almost fun. They sat around me in the dorm, all talking at once, throwing words and questions at me in rapid-fire succession. We all needed answers, and they expected conversation within minutes. But I couldn't oblige.

They would point to the floor in the general direction of my feet while they said, "shoes." I watched them in frustration; I asked myself if they thought I had big feet or, were they asking me to stand up?

After a time, as if it would help me understand better, they talked louder. Did they think I was hard of hearing? Even when they were nearly shouting, I had no idea what they wanted when they pointed at me: my name, my turn to speak, the color of my blouse, or, did I have dirt on my nose?

It didn't take long for the first blush of enthusiasm to wane. Their let's-go-see-what-the-new-French-girl-is-like excitement wore off; the novelty was soon gone. I was something different, an oddity to be stared at, to be touched, and finally, to be teased. This, they did with relish. When our imaginative brand of sign language lost its luster, they lost interest. And I lost hope.

English confounded me. What a messy and complicated language, I thought. Cumbersome complex rules, too many exceptions, words of multiple meanings and strange pronunciation drove me crazy.

No, the word "close" does not necessarily mean something you wear, nor does it always suggest nearness, neither does "hair" mean the opposite of "there," nor does "pee" mean a legume you eat. Also, when does "I" mean "eye," and "fall" not mean you're clumsy? And how in Heaven's name am I supposed to know that my ice cream dessert isn't spelled "deyzzurt?" Then, there was the snide, "*Wazzamadda, duntcheggittit?*"

No, Smarty, I do not get it!

Why, oh why didn't anybody here know anything other than English, preferably something with a Latin base? Everyone else I had ever known was multi-lingual. I was frustrated beyond words.

After several solitary weeks, however, I decided I couldn't live like this any longer. I absolutely needed to break out of my language prison. I reasoned that if everyone here had learned to speak English, so could I. Failure was not an option.

So I set about practicing certain awkward but typical sounds that I heard frequently. I immediately ran into trouble; my tongue would simply not do my bidding. It did not know those tricky maneuvers toward the front of my mouth. After all, let's be fair; it had never lived there. My native Latin-based French pronunciation system was rooted in the romantic recesses found at the rear of my mouth, in the dark, mysterious regions of my throat. So was my Yiddish-as-a-second-language, as well as the smattering of Spanish I had quickly learned. What lingual contortions English required!

My initial efforts were near disasters. I found certain English words nearly impossible to pronounce. I kept trying but always with the same results. My efforts were apparently entertaining to my cottage mates. After a time, they even thought I might be fracturing their language deliberately.

Mocking began. Wherever I went, teasing followed about the funny way I spoke and the nickname, "Frenchy" soon spread beyond our cottage. Had it not been for the pejorative tone I detected in their voices, I would probably have borne that name with pride. But I couldn't bear it because "Frenchy," like a deadly missile, was aimed at wounding me; and it did hurt, horribly. I wanted so much to fit in, to belong. But my nickname was a constant reminder that I was unacceptably different from my peers.

How cruel they were. They had great fun tormenting me. First, they laughed at my clumsiness. Next, they called me names, which made me cry. Then, they jeered, "Crybaby! Crybaby!"

Crying was something I did frequently in those early days. My adjustment period was one of intense culture shock and vulnerability. I was nearly distraught with worry over my parents, and I missed them desperately. I tried to convey to my cottage sisters what I felt, that life under the Nazis had caused me pain unlike any other, and to please not hurt me any more and be patient with me while I learned their language. My efforts were a disaster. They misunderstood and only teased and jeered all the more. They were, after all, still children, I told myself. How could they understand what it was like to be hunted by real human demons and to lose everything that was the very essence of your life?

For all intents and purposes, I was alone once more. But I did not give up. I would lie awake at night, long after everyone else had gone to sleep, and practice in my head over and over again the word sounds that I had been unable to utter during the day.

I tried to reconcile the way my French eyes saw words such as "vegetable" printed on paper--each syllable and letter clearly and consistently pronounced--with what my ears heard from my peers. They would say, vetchtbl" accenting the first syllable and swallowing the rest. But, wait! Wasn't the word, "table" pronounced with a long "a?" Yes, it was. So, I came up with, "veh-djeh-'TĀY-buhll" accenting the second-last syllable. Charming, but totally wrong.

I also held long, silent discussions with myself about these and other woes of the day, especially the teasing and taunting from my peers. In my head, in my private French world, I got even. There, I found great comfort at being quite candid and graphic with the purveyors of such woes about their despicable behavior. I visualized giving them articulate scathing lectures about needing to grow up. Then, I felt much better.

Finally, before trying to go to sleep, I prayed that my maman and papa were safe and we would soon be reunited--I missed them so. This last routine was accompanied by a nightly bout of tears.

As time went on, I withdrew further into my private world, the only place where my nickname, the teasing, and the hurting would not follow. Once again I hid my feelings from the world and became too tough for anyone to hurt me anymore. I was determined to survive this episode in my life.

#

A Yiddish-speaking social worker was assigned to be our caseworker. I believe her name was Claire Meyers. There were weekly visits at first, sometimes more. We spent many hours talking. Her large, caring, gray eyes stayed with me long after our visits were over. We came to know each other well. She became my confidante. We spoke openly, as one adult to another, Miss Meyers and I. I told her all my problems, and my worries over my parents.

I hungered for information. The one or two censored letters I had received from my mother since my arrival usually asked how my sisters and I were doing and scolded me for not writing more often. Nothing was ever said about how they were doing. I wanted to know the direction of the War, and how Maman and Papa were doing in Barcelona. I knew that the agency was in touch with "The Joint," over there, so I asked Miss Meyers a lot of questions about my parents.

I was also curious about the progress being made to find us a foster home. And, who was paying for our care since my parents could not?

From her answer, I finally understood what the word "welfare" meant; my pride was badly bruised. Although I understood why it had to be, I nevertheless felt humiliated and embarrassed. My parents had told me about the unfortunates who sometimes had nothing on which to live; everyone pitied them and sometimes threw money at them--like I used to throw crumbs at birds in the park.

If my Bellefaire peers ever found out, this would be one more thing for them to tease about (though it is likely they were all on welfare too). I felt terribly self-conscious and exposed. So from then on, I did everything I could to hide the fact that I was on welfare. During the years that followed, only my closest, most trusted adult friends knew.

Miss Meyers and I also talked about how difficult it was to find a foster family willing and able to care for three children. There were pros and cons to all the choices we faced. Then there was this damnable language barrier to consider too. Not many Cleveland families spoke Yiddish; and virtually none spoke French. There were families willing to take one child, or perhaps two. But three were too great a burden for most foster homes. So, I made another decision. I told her I wanted the two little ones to be kept together at any cost.

"They are very close, and they need each another. If you can't find a home for all three of us, then please first find a place for them together in one home." I wanted to be with them as long as possible. "If I leave Bellefaire before they do, there will be no one here who can speak their language."

Miss Meyers was an excellent, empathetic listener. She understood; a home was found fairly quickly for the girls. By the time they left the orphanage in the early fall of 1943, they had already picked up the rudiments of English. They would be able to make themselves understood. I remained at Bellefaire a while longer. Miss Meyers came occasionally all the way from her downtown office to pick me up in her car so we could go visit the girls together.

After the girls left, I was terribly lonely. My cottage sisters were now in school and I was left alone. I wanted to go back to school too but my language skills were still inadequate; and my instructional needs had to be assessed for proper grade placement. In the fall, I was given an aptitude test. This test was, of course, in English. Unsurprisingly, language comprehension was found to be my biggest problem.

Based on the test results, I was assigned one-on-one English language instruction. Miss Meyers told me this concentrated tutoring would produce faster results. She said there was a school in Cleveland Heights where such attention could be given me, and I would be driven there and back for my lessons. So far, it sounded okay.

Unfortunately, this small school was actually a facility for mentally retarded children. I had already started there when this fact sank in. I was appalled. All kinds of thoughts ran through my head. My test scores are too low? Is that the real reason I have to go to a school for the mentally retarded? What's wrong with me, didn't I learn well enough in my French schools? What else is in store? What other degradation waits for me?

I took this as an extremely insulting demotion given the academic recognition I had enjoyed in the elementary school of my own country. Was my French education worthless here? Didn't they know I had received awards for superior achievement in Reading and Arithmetic? So what if the reading had been in French! [9] My bruised ego worked hard at defending itself. Me? Attend a school for mentally retarded children? I was incredulous!

Then, panic! What will my cottage mates make of this information when it reaches their ears? Oh, how they'll regale in the fun to be had at my expense if they ever find out.

But it did motivate me to apply myself more. When I told Miss Meyers how I felt, she assured me my tutoring lessons in that school had nothing whatever to do with my native abilities. It was the only facility where staff was available for special one on one instruction. She agreed to keep this information just between us and to make sure the cottage mother maintained the utmost discretion as well. To my great relief, my cottage sisters never learned of my academic embarrassment.

The fall of 1943 wore on. Every day I was taken by bus to my tutoring session. I learned fast, but I didn't always want to let on. I discovered there were certain advantages to not having people know exactly how much I understood. In the pre-teen, somewhat lazy phase that I was approaching, I often found it useful to look uncomprehending when I was asked to do certain chores at my Bellefaire home. And it worked! As a foreigner who was given degrading status, this was a convenient perk; I felt fully justified exploiting it. This is justice, I told myself. I had turned a major liability into an asset. My father would have approved.

At last, it came about that I could speak enough English to get by. The day was finally here for me to enroll in a normal school. The last time I had attended such a school was in the fall of 1942 when I was hidden in my farmhouse home in southern France. In Spain and Portugal, I had not had any formal instruction.

---

9   Knowledge of these early awards did not undo the damage to my self-esteem left by the implicit message of going to a school for the mentally retarded. Those bruises took years to heal.

And, after my arrival in Cleveland, it was deemed necessary to first give me more time to master English.

When the time came to determine my grade, my caseworker, in consultation with educators, decided to further ease the pressures of learning a new language. They built into my academic placement an additional year for me to learn English before throwing new abstract concepts at me. Since I had already missed one year in Europe, this meant that when I was finally enrolled in my first American school, instead of being placed in the eighth grade with my peers, I was put two years behind them, in the sixth--another blow to my ego. What else is to come my way?

Meantime, a foster home had been found for me. When I learned where it was located, I was delighted because, per my request to Miss Meyers, this home was within walking distance of my sisters' foster home. Now I could really keep an eye on their welfare and development as I had sworn to do.

Indeed, many times, when I visited them, I found myself teaching them good manners like Maman would have done. I also admonished them when bad physical habits began to form so that they would grow straight, speak without a lisp, or walk without waddling. Maman expected these things of me. Furthermore, since we now all attended the same elementary school, I could also be their defender.

They still spoke with a slight accent, as did I. Teasing was expected, especially from boys who sometimes went too far. At such times, I had to take corrective action. Fortunately, Mother Nature was on my side. Being older and taller than all the kids in school, and being a tomboy who had become tough emotionally as well as physically, I had a distinct advantage. I wasn't going to take any guff from anybody.

Soon, many a boy learned the hard way that you don't mess around with the Grossman girls. The price was usually a most painful and well-placed kick. True, this was unladylike behavior, but what choice did I have? However, sooner or later, such socially incorrect behavior was bound to attract the attention of the school principal.

One day, during a recess, Eveline came to me, in tears. Some bully fourth-grader had gotten out of line with her and Paulette because of the funny way they spoke. She said the boy was at that very moment still picking on Paulette. Furious, I ran down the school's three flights of stairs, two steps at a time, to confront the wrongdoer. Paulette, cornered by a big fat boy taunting her, was crying uncontrollably by now.

"Stop! Leave my sister alone." I ordered in my limited English and shoved him aside to comfort Paulette.

"Make me." was the boy's response and this chubby bully, using a badly distorted version of my own French accent, now turned his taunting toward me.

Big mistake!

An all-out battle followed. After all, what boy could let a mere girl tell him what to do? We pummeled each other and rolled around on the floor while a growing crowd of boys gathered, yelling encouragement to their buddy. But this good-for-nothing bully who had made my little sisters cry was now getting a hefty dose of what he deserved; he was no longer laughing.

A large crowd of children--girls as well as boys--gathered within a few minutes. The girls, always willing to align themselves against the boys, cheered me on. This only made the boys more vocal in their support of the bully. The shouts and screams from the crowd became nearly deafening.

I had just gotten a firm judo-like grip around his neck and arms after kicking him in the shins, when the tumult drew the attention of the teaching staff. Disheveled as we were, we were both taken to the principal's office to face the consequences. I immediately took charge. In my halting English and convincing accent, I explained the cause of the ruckus and pointed to my weeping little sister who had followed me.

Despite the damage to my now tearful adversary, I was given a relatively light scolding, whereas the bully was appropriately admonished for his lack of sensitivity and poor citizenship. He never troubled us again.

And my oath to Maman continued to be honored.

#

This oath hung over my head like a dark and heavy cloud; it was never far from my thoughts. I worried constantly about whether I was doing a good enough job. Some time in the spring of 1944, providence gave me the opportunity to once again take action in my sisters' lives.

Some weeks after I began visiting them in their foster home, it became apparent that the girls were too big a challenge for their foster mother. They had become hyperactive little hellions who knew nothing of limits. It was obvious to me, even as young as I was, that their emotional adjustment had not followed the hoped-for course.

Since early 1943, and following the separation from their natural parents, they had had sketchy supervision, inconsistent guidance, and haphazard discipline. Unfortunately, the very opposite was needed; and the language barrier only aggravated the problem. Misbehavior was predictable.

Their foster mother did not know how to cope with them other than to rely on overly zealous spankings in an effort to gain obedience. They, for their part, conspired creatively to get even with her. One such tactic was drawing pictures with toothpaste on the brand new wallpaper of their bedroom, an artistic endeavor undertaken during one of the times they were grounded there.

The girls probably did deserve a solid spanking now and then. However, the ones they got were a bit too solid. Bruise marks were sometimes left on the girls' arms and legs. Their foster mother had obviously crossed the line between discipline and abuse.

When the girls complained to me on one of my visits in late spring, and showed me their bruises, I decided this home was not in my sisters' best interests. Even though Maman and Papa had been strict disciplinarians, they would not approve either. I did not intend to be untrue to my oath, and decided it was time to get my sisters out of there!

So I went home and phoned Miss Meyers. During our meeting that week, I told her what I had seen and passionately asked that my sisters be moved to another home. She promised to investigate.

I undoubtedly made a pest of myself by calling her often to see what progress she was making. But, it finally paid off. In August, the girls were removed from this foster home and readmitted to Bellefaire. The official reason given, I learned years later, was that the foster mother had become ill and could no longer care for young children. In my letters to Maman, I never told her the real reason; I didn't want her to worry.

Several months went by before another home was found. Fortunately, the new foster family was far better suited to the girls' special needs. Though their new home was now somewhat distant from my own, I was still able to visit them often by bus and I could tell they were much happier there. They developed a lasting fondness for their new surrogate parents.

As for me, I was the most fortunate of all. My foster family paved the way to my future. It gave me the kind of value base and firm foundation upon which I later felt very comfortable building much of my life. I had a foster grandpa, foster uncles, and foster cousins who were part of my everyday experience. My foster parents, Hilda and Ed Jaffe, were truly caring people who gave me a sense of belonging. They made me feel that I was as important to them as they were to me. We became a close family.

Hilda was a kind, generous and strong woman who became an invaluable role model for me when I had no viable alternatives.

She understood the burdens I carried and treated me like an adult. Innately sensitive to the delicate nature of the role she played in my life as a surrogate parent, she never attempted to replace my mother in my heart. Our relationship was truly special.

A deep, permanent bond grew out of the times we shared together and we became lifelong friends. I was indeed fortunate to have a second Maman who loved me and nurtured me as if I had been her own. I called her, "Mom."

We were now at last, all three of us safe and well cared-for, my little sisters and I.

"*Tu vois, Maman?* I did it! I kept my oath to you."

The End? Not Yet.

CHAPTER XVII

The Legacy

After I settled in my foster home, I worked hard at honing my new language skills. My foster mom was extremely supportive and spent a lot of time helping me with pronunciation and spelling. Within a year, I mastered the rudiments of English. Once I had overcome my early pronunciation problems, the nickname, "Frenchy," became irrelevant and, in a short time, it was no longer used. Thank God, the teasing was finally over. I now blended in and became a totally American girl.

Without the accent to remind my peers I was a "greenhorn" and because I didn't discuss my background anymore, in time, most people forgot I was French. New classmates knew nothing about me; even my teachers didn't know I was a recent arrival to their country, and I made no effort to change that. In fact, I consciously avoided the subject. Without realizing it, I was again hiding and protecting myself by continuing the pattern of behavior that began in 1940: keeping my mouth shut about myself. Instead of hiding from physical threat, I was now hiding from emotional pain. In time, this hiding became second nature.

Intent on catching up to my age group in school, every term from then on, I signed up for extra courses, and every summer, I enrolled in summer school. This way I eventually earned enough credits to make up the years I had lost, and was able to graduate with my rightful high school class.

#

When the war ended in Europe, my parents immediately returned to France from Barcelona, where they had safely waited for the end of the war. Their first stop was Luchon to retrieve their buried records and family treasures, intact, from the backyard of Josie Kirsch Cohen's home.

Upon their return to Paris, they found their condominium apartment had been expropriated by Vichy and stripped bare of all their belongings. Their expensive furnishings and factory equipment were all gone. They tried to get compensation from the French government for the loss of their property but, at the time, their efforts were useless and were met with vehement denials of responsibility. Nevertheless, with the little that remained of what they had managed to hide in Luchon, and with the help of a few renewed contacts, Simon and Anna were able to re-establish a business in Paris--though considerably scaled down from the one they had prior to their 1940 departure.

Meanwhile, in the United States, I had kept abreast of world events. I knew when the war was ending. I expected and eagerly anticipated being reunited with my parents quickly when the war was over. As the end approached, I became so excited; I couldn't wait to return to Paris. Shortly after the surrender, I made enquiries of my caseworker about returning to my native country. She told me that we could return to our homeland without further delay when our parents made the necessary arrangements for a chaperone. However, she could not say if, or when, our parents themselves could come to the United States if that was what they preferred to do. This depended on their decisions, and on the United States' visitor and immigration quotas.

I missed my parents deeply. In 1945, I was nearly fourteen. Following our two-year separation, I longed desperately to return to my native country, to the home of my cherished childhood and to my beloved family. I wrote my parents and begged them to come for my sisters and me, or to send for us if they could not come. I felt that the two years our lives had been on hold while the war raged on was long enough. But, the expense of making the round-trip crossing as visitors was more than my parents felt they could afford, and entry visas for immigration were not being readily given to Polish Jews.

I was annoyed and restless. Privately, I had clung to my French identity and had bided my time until I could return to my birthplace. But my father--still hoping to fulfill his life-long dream of immigrating to the United States--had more complex priorities. He was working hard to save enough money for a fresh start in America.

I began to feel that my sisters and I were paying a dear price for our father's dream, and I became resentful. Though I understood the logic of his thinking, I totally disagreed with his decision not to place the reuniting of our family above all other considerations. I reasoned that if he felt compelled to remain in Paris for a while longer to strengthen the family's financial position, why couldn't my mother come by herself to get my sisters and me following the end of hostilities in 1945? We could all be together in Paris while they waited for their immigration papers. But, perhaps, by remaining in the United States, we served as added leverage for them in obtaining visas from the U.S. Immigration Service.

#

It took another two years beyond the German surrender, until late fall of 1947, before our family reunion took place. By then, we had been separated from our parents for four and a half years. Eveline, Paulette and I had grown up a great deal and become fully acculturated in that time. I continued to harbor resentment at having had to wait so long, but when I heard my parents were finally on their way, I put my resentment aside. All three of us were incredibly excited and proud. We were going to be able to show everyone at long last, that we did, indeed, have parents.

I was still living in my original foster home when they arrived in the United States. Knowing how eager I was to see them, my foster mother took me to New York so that I could be there to greet my parents upon their arrival at the pier. I was surprised that my mother, who had been teaching herself

English in France, knew enough to be able to communicate on a basic level with my foster mother. I was so proud of her.

That day, I finally saw the Statue of Liberty. It seemed fitting that we, Papa, Maman and I, see this symbol of new hope together. My family was now reunited, happy and so very hopeful. Our future looked bright.

But new demons awaited.

#

Before we all moved in together again in Cleveland, there was a changeover period during which time certain legal issues of responsibility for our care had to be finalized by the Jewish Family Service. We were to remain in our foster parents' homes until that time. This imposed transition gave my father a chance to investigate business opportunities and to evaluate his prospects in Cleveland. In the meantime, our parents came to spend time with us nearly every day.

After a short while, temporary living arrangements were made for our parents so we could spend weekends alone with them. We talked about many things. Before long, philosophical disagreements surfaced. I began to suspect that we might not have the happy ending of which I had so often dreamed.

On many occasions, we locked horns. Our family's opposing cultures seemed to be on collision course. My father's discussions with my mother often raised the possibility that we might all go back to France permanently. This kind of talk got my immediate attention. I wasn't ready for that ending anymore. Two years earlier, at the end of the war, my suitcase would have been packed before a word was said. But now, I wanted to remain in Cleveland long enough to graduate high school and get my diploma.

The nearly five years our family had been separated had spanned a critical period in our childhood development. It was too long for an easy transition to take place. We had become strangers.

For my part, I found that the Maman and Papa I had left five years earlier had not adjusted to the passage of time. Perhaps they had subconsciously expected to be met by the same child. But the little girl that Simon and Anna had sent away with two babies in her charge was no more. In 1943, they had entrusted that eleven-year-old, with adult responsibilities and had expected her to behave accordingly. Now, in 1948, they wanted to pick things up where they left off. But I, at sixteen, expected to be treated the way others now treated me, as a young adult accustomed to responsibility and to making her own decisions. These differing expectations set our family dynamics in confrontation mode.

One factor that contributed to the tension between us was our parents' insistence on running their household and family the French way: firmly patriarchal, with far more discipline than the American family model that they believed to be too permissive. Our interactions quickly became a strain on everyone. For me, adjustments meant either total capitulation or absolute resistance. Most of the time it had to be absolute resistance, because give and take were not in Simon's mind-set when it came to his daughter. Negotiations were out of the question.

When my father tried to convince me to quit high school, for example, I knew this was not going to end well. He felt that since I had learned to sew and had become fairly adept at making my own clothes, I should drop out of school and become a dressmaker. He saw this as a practical way to ease the pressure on our family finances. I "would start earning money right away and contribute to the family income." That's the way it was done in France and that's the way it would be done in this household, he declared.

I disagreed. We had long, heated discussions on the importance of a high school diploma. My parents' cultural loyalty and values were still aligned with those of France where many students only went through an eighth grade equivalent in school before going on into a vocational or trades program. I, on the other hand, was now fiercely loyal to my adopted country and touted its educational values. I had other plans. I was nearly seventeen years old and knew my own mind. I wanted to finish high school and get my diploma. If I were ever to go to college, I would need my diploma, I said. My hopes and dreams had been shaped by my American experience during a pivotal developmental period of my life.

We became an almost dysfunctional family. Of course, the war was responsible. But, within its context, two related factors played a major role: first, at war's end, my parents' top priority was understandably to reestablish an income stream; second, the United States' post-war limits on immigration quotas did not take into account the humanitarian issues of our unique family situation. So, instead of the joy Simon and Anna should have found in interactions with their eldest, they were greeted with confusion, anger, bitterness and strife.

After a few months of evaluating his options in this new world of his daughter's, Simon returned to France. His temporary visa had expired, and he was now no longer certain the United States was where he wanted to settle with his family. Besides, in order to keep his business operating in Paris, he needed to go back and tend to it personally.

My mother, unwilling to leave us again, chose to remain while I continued high school. She applied for, and was able to obtain, the necessary immigration documents to remain in the United States.

So, even after the war ended, our wrenching family separations continued, one of the many tragic legacies of that nightmarish period. But at least the arguments over my high school diploma stopped--for now.

#

Maman rented an apartment in Cleveland. The girls and I were transferred from the care of our foster parents to our mother's, and we all set up housekeeping together. Since our new home was very close to the girls' former one and within the same school district, they did not have to change schools. But, when I moved from the Jaffes' to my mother's home, I changed school districts and high schools.

There were many obstacles for the family to overcome, not the least of which were resources on which to live. Good-paying jobs were not available to my mother, whose English skills were not considered strong enough; she could only find menial factory work. The money my father left her ran out and she was obliged to apply for aid from the Jewish Assistance program. Once more, I was on welfare, the humiliating place in which I had never, ever wanted to be again.

This period was a difficult one for all of us, but especially for our mother. Now, although she was working, she did not earn enough to support us. Being a "single" head of household, thousands of miles away from her husband for an undetermined amount of time, must have taken a great toll on her. But, being a family again was perhaps the most painful adjustment for her; the transition was never fully successful, and she was guilt-ridden. She had already paid a dear price for sending her children away five years earlier. The loss of those years, during her exile in Barcelona, left deep scars. She began to have mood swings and occasionally suffered from bouts of deep depression. Within a year, these episodes became severe enough that she was counseled to seek medical help. Doctors diagnosed her as having "involutional melancholia."

Letters went back and forth across our continents. At some point, my parents decided that France was, after all, to be our true home. My mother announced to us that we were all to return to Paris. My father was well known and respected there, and an income source was already well established. He could support us well there.

Ironically, after lifelong efforts to immigrate to the United States, he no longer wanted to do so. His self-confidence had flagged. He'd seen how difficult it would be for him, at fifty-one years of age, to start anew. He had no command of English, no familiarity with the ways and institutions of American business, and few friends or contacts to pave the way. His ego needed the re-enforcement afforded him in France, where he was known by many, admired by some, and respected by all who did business with him. In France, Simon Grossman was somebody; in the United States, he was a 'nobody.'

So, in late summer of 1949, my father returned to the United States to bring his family back to France. He wanted us with him right away. I was devastated. By that time, it meant even more to me to finish high school and I was so close to realizing my goal. Furthermore, I now also had a serious boyfriend, a boy from my old neighborhood whom I had met when I first moved in with the Jaffes. We had started dating when I was fifteen. Love blossomed quickly between us and had grown during the years that followed our first date. I had recently accepted his college fraternity pin, the closest thing to being engaged (without the ring), and I was in no mood to return it, or to give up my diploma.

Arguments over my high school education started anew. After all, of what use would this education be to a woman in France, he said. I feared that his old-world attitudes would always be obstacles to my achieving my full potential. My dreams even included the possibility of attending the École des Beaux Arts in Paris. An American high school diploma would be expected, I told him. I was determined to get that diploma! There were many angry exchanges over this issue. But I stood my ground. At eighteen, I was no longer intimidated by my father and was ready to run away if need be. He knew he was defeated.

So, in the fall of 1949, my parents returned to their Paris home with only two of their three daughters. The Jewish Family Service of Cleveland came to our rescue once more and found me a temporary foster home close to my old high school so that I could finish my studies. Six months later, in June 1950, with great satisfaction and pride, I walked up to the podium to receive my diploma. That summer, I joined my parents and my sisters in France.

#

Upon my arrival in Paris, I found my grandfather Avram Gielcman in failing health. Despite his ill health, we spent a lot of time together and recaptured some of the warmth of earlier years. I felt fortunate to be by his side on November 1 when he passed away. He had so very much wanted me to return to Paris so that he could see me again. As sad as his loss left me, I was grateful that I had been able to put my arms around him once more and to brighten his final days by making one of his last wishes come true.

Now that I was back in France, I discovered that, though I still adored the city of my birth, I found it was no longer enough for me. There was another love in my life that I had left behind in the United States, the boy from Cleveland. Unsurprisingly, several months after my return to Paris, my heart beckoned me back. In spring 1951, we were married.

Meanwhile, in the totally French household I had left behind in Paris where my sisters now lived, two stormy years followed. There was little family harmony. The girls missed their oldest sister--who was no longer there to take their side in family squabbles--and they missed their American ways. They complained continually, and put constant pressure on their parents to return to America. My mother added pressures of her own. She wanted to have all three of her children near her. There was no peace for anyone.

My father again had to make a painful decision. In 1952, he finally capitulated and liquidated his business. The once brave, would-be stow-away of earlier times, at last immigrated legally to the United States. However, the occasion did not generate the enthusiasm and joy it would have at one time.

Sadly, now much older and set in his ways, he never recovered completely from a pernicious case of culture shock. At fifty-four, he could not fully adjust to his new identity in America. In that new world, he saw himself as a 'nobody.' He and my mother initially settled in Cleveland where my sisters graduated high school. Then, they moved to Philadelphia. Ten years later, my father died there, a disillusioned man, of a diseased and broken heart.

His death left my mother without the pillar of strength and control on which she had come to lean. In their later years, she had increasingly emulated him and in many distorted, sometimes grotesque ways, she had become a mirror image of him. She behaved like him, and even sounded like him. But she lacked his emotional strength and courage. These were personal attributes she had lost during the war and during her many years as a highly controlled spouse. Following his death, she was unable to rebuild her life.

Too many of the painful decisions she had made during wartime and in the early post-war years, had set the stage for the personal conflicts that continued to develop between her and her daughters. As a result, we grew apart. But all the while, her needs kept increasing. She was obsessed with a desire for love and attention from us. She now wanted to be the center of our universes. We would have had to surrender our own personal and family needs to accommodate hers. We nevertheless tried to give as much as we could, sometimes at great emotional cost to our families and ourselves. It was futile. Due to the nature of her psychological condition, "severe chronic melancholia," her needs were insatiable. No matter what we did or how much we gave of ourselves, it would never be enough.

Who could have guessed that the beautiful and talented young woman of the 1920s, so full of life and full of hope, would die alone in a mental health-care facility, the personification of wretchedness. At seventy-one, by continuously hitting her head against a wall, she finally succeeded in giving chase to the demons that haunted her adult life, the tragic legacy of a horrible war that tore her family and her life apart.

#

Having children of my own, I understand the desperate choices that my parents faced. I still disagree with some of their decisions, yet without them, the richly rewarding life and successful careers I have had, with my Cleveland soul mate by my side, could not have been mine. Undoubtedly, it was because of those difficult early years that I became a strong, fiercely independent person with a passion for life, an unquenchable thirst for learning and an abiding love of family.

I now also embrace my ethnic legacy openly. Though there were a great many years during my adulthood when I continued to hide who and what I was, a foreign-born and despised Jew, I have learned to respect the rich heritage into which I was born. I come from a people whose resilience and strength are legendary and whose humanity, philanthropy and contributions in all fields of human endeavor are exemplary. I bear this heritage with pride, to be passed on to future generations.

Yet, deep down in the most sheltered, most private recesses of my soul, I still carry a demon or two. Though I have banished many of them, ghosts of earlier times reappear now and then. To forget what was taken from the happy family that once was mine is out of the question. I have never stopped mourning my lost childhood. And to forgive what I cannot forget is simply too abstract a question for me to face. I still feel vulnerable. The wariness, the fear, the impulse to hide or look over my shoulder, these survival instincts of the ten-year-old I once was, will always haunt me.

THE END

CHASED BY DEMONS: ©
How I Survived Hitler's Madness In My Native France

BY

JACQUELINE GROSSMAN

ADDITIONAL

SOURCES AND
REFERENCES

SOURCES AND REFERENCES

Institutional Archives and Libraries

Archives of the Jewish Joint Distribution Committee - New York, New York

Archives of the Bellefaire Jewish Children's Bureau – Cleveland, Ohio

The Holocaust Center of Northern California - San Francisco, California

United States Holocaust Memorial Museum Library – Washington DC

United States National Archives - Washington DC

Western Reserve Historical Society: Cleveland Jewish Archives, Jewish Children's Bureau, 1940-46 – Cleveland, Ohio

Publications

Aux Frontières de la Liberté, Robert Belot – Paris, Fayard, 1998

La Vie des Français Sous l'Occupation, Henri Amouroux – Arthème, Fayard, 1961

Les Passeurs 1943: Une Épopée Tragique, Susel et Olivier Nadouce

The Jews of France, Esther Benbassa (Transl. M.B. DeBevoise)

The Jews of Modern France, Paula E. Hyman

The Jews of Paris and the Final Solution, Jacques Adler – Oxford University Press, 1987

The Mezuzzah in the Madonna's Foot, Trudi Alexy – Simon & Shuster, 1993

Paris Allemand, Henri Michel, A. Michel, 1981

Sauver les Enfants, Vivette Samuel

Visas to Freedom: The History of HIAS, Mark Wischnitzer – Cleveland, World Publishing Company, 1956

CPSIA information can be obtained at www.ICGtesting.com
Printed in the USA
BVOW010349081112

304979BV00005B/1/P